FRAMING FILM is a book series dedicated to
theoretical and analytical studies in restoration,
collection, archival, and exhibition practices in line
with the existing archive of EYE Filmmuseum. With
this series, Amsterdam University Press and EYE aim
to support the academic research community, as well
as practitioners in archive and restoration.

CLAUDY OP DEN KAMP

THE GREATEST FILMS NEVER SEEN

The Film Archive and the Copyright Smokescreen

AMSTERDAM UNIVERSITY PRESS

eye

Published by EYE Filmmuseum / Amsterdam University Press

Cover illustration: Stanley H. Durwood Film Vault, The Kansas City Public Library
(courtesy of Mike Sinclair)
Cover design and lay-out: Magenta Ontwerpers, Bussum

Previous versions of some of the chapters in this book have been published in Virginia Crisp
and Gabriel Menotti (eds.) (2015) *Besides the Screen: Moving Images Through Distribution,
Promotion and Curation*. London: Palgrave Macmillan; Matthew David and Debora Halbert
(eds.) (2014) *The SAGE Handbook of Intellectual Property*. London: SAGE Publications Ltd.; as
well as *Art Libraries Journal; ilinx. Berlin Journal for Cultural History and Theory; Provenance,
Journal of the Society of Georgia Archivists; International Association of Sound and Audiovisual
Archives (IASA) Journal;* and *UWA Law Review*.

PLYMOUTH UNIVERSITY

ISBN   978 94 6298 139 3
e-ISBN 978 90 4853 104 2
DOI   10.5117/9789462981393
NUR   670

TABLE OF CONTENTS

In loving memory of Martha Blassnigg (1968-2015)

ACKNOWLEDGEMENTS

It has been the pervasive and powerful kindness of many people that have made this book possible. The ideas underpinning this book originated at the Nederlands Filmmuseum, where I would like to thank my former colleagues, in particular Leontien Bout, Giovanna Fossati, Mark-Paul Meyer, and Walter Swagemakers. The work then came to fruition as a PhD at Plymouth University, where I would like to thank everyone at Transtechnology Research, and specifically Michael Punt. Writing the thesis happened during my time at the University of Zurich, where I would like to thank Barbara Flueckiger, Franziska Heller, David Pfluger, and Kristina Koehler for their support. I wrote the first revision during my time at Swinburne Law School, where I would like to thank Dan Hunter, Jessica Lake, and Amanda Scardamaglia. At Bournemouth University, where the work was revised into its current version, I would like to thank my colleagues on both the Film and CIPPM teams, in particular Maurizio Borghi and Dinusha Mendis. A special thank you goes to Michael Wilmore. At AUP, I would like to single out the support from Maryse Elliott and Frank Kessler. For interventions, contributions, and great conversations, I would like to thank Kathy Bowrey, Fran Cetti, Matthew David, Peter Decherney, Gustav Deutsch, Dennis Doros, Stef van Gompel, Just van der Hoeven, Peter Jaszi, Janna Jones, Martin Koerber, Mike Mashon, Bartolomeo Meletti, Eric Schwartz, Elizabeth Townsend Gard, Leenke Ripmeester, Lee Tsiantis, Andrea Wallace, with a special thank you to Ronan Deazley. On a personal level, there were many that cared for my sanity. I would like to acknowledge the support of Clarissa Almeida Ribeiro, Verónica Arnáiz Rivas, Naomi Birdthistle, Rita Cachão, Charlotte Coles, Angela Daly, Amanda Egbe, Karin van Es, Chantal van der Horst, Bregt Lameris, Eef Masson, Stefka Mueller, Simone Pyne, Elena Rossi-Snook, Ronny Temme, Paulien Wenting, and Tegan Zimmerman. Thank you...!

PREFACE

In *Buster Keaton Never Smiles*, Dutch author Arnon Grunberg devotes one of his essays to Martin Scorsese's documentary on Italian cinema. He argues that Scorsese's personal voyage through film demonstrates that the films you love, and that arguably help shape your emotional life, could be seen as an 'auto-biography'. I have always felt that to be true. However, I did not realize just how few titles comprise the formative years of my autobiography until I came across a 2016 article in *The New Yorker*, in which Tad Friend claims that the 'average teenager [...] sees six films a year in the [film] theatre'. I understand that media consumption in general, and cinema-going in particular, has changed tremendously over the last few decades, but this number astonished me, because it is closer to the *total* amount of films I saw in the cinema as a teenager.

My handful of cinema-going experiences (in addition to a youth spent glued to the television), however, were life-altering: not only did these moving-image experiences make me question the world, myself, and who I wanted to be, but also informed my later professional choices. This preface is the story of the films I was able to see, and perhaps more importantly, the ones I later dis-covered I could not. This discovery, and some of the reasons why I was unable to access these films, form part of the personal and professional experiences that serve as the background to this book.

'LET'S START AT THE VERY BEGINNING'

In the autumn of 1994, during one of my first film history classes at the Univer-sity of Amsterdam, we were shown Peter Delpeut's LYRISCH NITRAAT ('LYRI-CAL NITRATE', 1990). I am quite sure it must have been a fuzzy VHS copy of the

THE PICTURE IDOL (US 1912, Dir. James Young)
(courtesy of EYE Film Institute)

film, but I was mesmerized. My previous experience of silent film had been limited to television screenings, and mainly consisted of – with all due respect – Laurel and Hardy. So, 'studying' a film that used non-slapstick, 'lyrical' silent film footage, woven into a story, was a revelation. Shortly afterwards, I went on a class excursion to Overveen, a beautiful Dutch seaside resort, where the Nederlands Filmmuseum's nitrate film vaults are located. This visit took place at a time when I fully subscribed to the 'myth of the archive as a repository of objective truth where documents lay dormant, waiting to be roused' (Amad, 2010, p. 159); this was where the film had been assembled, and the magical location where the inflammable clips resided.

It was the spectacular final scene of LYRISCH NITRAAT, in particular, that hit home. In this scene from Edward Warren's WARFARE OF THE FLESH (1917), in which Adam and Eve are expelled from the Garden of Eden, a flickering pattern of decaying nitrate slowly replaces the photographic image. As a viewer, your attention constantly shifts from the film's content to its surface as the decaying nitrate obstructs the narrative flow. The photographic images are overtaken by the irreversible process of decay, until the strip of film itself becomes the principal focus. Aside from the ambiguous emotion of enjoying the strange beauty of deteriorating film, the nostalgic sense of a (literally) disappearing cinema touched me deeply. I am only able to compare it to knowing your way around a house that does not exist anymore; watching the film filled me with a somewhat hallucinatory feeling. At some point, films, if they are not preserved, can no longer be seen, and if they cannot be seen, it will become increasingly hard to remember them. The vital force of past cinema will be permanently lost. As I watched Adam and Eve banished from their paradise, I too was expelled from mine.

'I'LL BE RIGHT HERE'

I ended up working in Overveen, as an archivist. Fortunately, my daily work in the film archive was not always as overwhelming as that first experience. Film preservation is, in the main, entertaining and fulfilling (albeit time-consuming) work, often culminating in a festive, champagne-filled film première. The realization that spending your days in this manner could be considered 'work' is still a little mind-boggling. My experience in Overveen involved working alongside highly motivated colleagues with a shared passion for everything film-related. Added to this was the regular excitement of receiving international guests, including academics and (found-footage) filmmakers, who were engaged in fascinating research projects. My 'work' also included frequent pilgrimages to Italy – to Le Giornate del Cinema Muto ('Pordenone Silent Film

Festival') in Pordenone and Il Cinema Ritrovato ('Cinema Rediscovered') in Bologna – where it took on an international perspective.

Mainly, however, I felt privileged to be able to view and engage with material that most people outside of the film archive world would probably never see. Over time, working in an environment where, as Peter Delpeut (1997, p. 7) put it so well, 'the marginal is the norm', questions began to creep up on me. What is it that is kept in the (public-sector) film archive? How does this enormous quantity of 'stuff' actually end up there? And how does what is kept and safeguarded in the archive relate to textbook film history? I have sensed the wonder and amazement that a few frames of film can elicit, and have happened across many mysterious faces along the way. Indeed, what I encountered in my archival practice had very little to do with the 'official' film history I had been taught. The biggest wonder was that I recognized almost none of these works.

'NOBODY PUTS BABY IN A CORNER'

The relationship between film historiography and film archives, and between the available filmic sources and their 'potential for history making' (Jones, 2012, p. 119) in particular, have fascinated me ever since. I pursued these reflections on the practical nature of archival work in the form of an MA in Film Archiving at the University of East Anglia. All elements of the degree, including the production of a creative product incorporating archival material, fostered my growing concern with the question of access to archival film.

An interest in archival access goes hand-in-hand with a desire to discover those factors that facilitate or impede it. There are, of course, issues of funding, language, and culture, as well of formats and technical obsolescence, but it was the legal factors that captured my interest the most. It was in the Brussels chapter of the Archimedia programme, in 1998, that I first came across the topic that would come to dominate my research interests, but it was in the practical archival environment that I really became aware of the intertwined relationship between copyright and access to archival collections.

My internship for the MA was spent in the sales department of the Nederlands Filmmuseum, where I coproduced a DVD entitled, *Highlights from the Collections*. Due to the nature of its content, rights clearance and a close collaboration with the museum's legal department played a major role in its production. My thesis centred on a Dutch film, whose release on DVD, it was predicted, would be significantly delayed, as the film's rights holders could not be traced. Today, the film would be regarded as an 'orphan work'.

'SHE RESCUES HIM RIGHT BACK'

My practical awareness of the burgeoning 'orphan works problem' resulted in a PhD research proposal for the Transtechnology Research Group at Plymouth University. Focusing on theoretical research, away from archival practice, provided me with the distance I needed to investigate the intricate relationship between the film archive and copyright. Initially, I thought of copyright as an exclusively restrictive concept. During the course of my research, however, I began to regard it in a subtler fashion as a filter that helps shape access to archival film in ways that both impede *and* facilitate. The resulting PhD thesis forms the basis of this book, which is partially informed by my theoretical and practical professional experiences.

On a personal level, the book is also the story of my changing relationship with the moving image. It is over 20 years since I first saw LYRISCH NITRAAT; meanwhile, I have turned into a person who now sees *more* films in the film theatre than the aforementioned 'average teenager'. And, of course, the options for viewing films have rapidly expanded. That one particular film, however, still fascinates: over time it has come to mean so many different things to me. Although my PhD research was firmly embedded in an academic context, I also relied on my experience of working inside a national public film archive – LYRISCH NITRAAT's wonderfully and provocatively compiled source material has helped me trace my memories of and access to that institute. In the meantime, the 'myth of the archive as a repository of objective truth' has evolved, for me, into a firm belief in the archive as a mediator of the past.

This book is a personal interpretation of what it means to think, to create, and to participate in a specific culture, and reminds me of my formative cinema-going years. In writing it, I have gained a deeper understanding of a certain 'permission culture', and the meaning of the ever-expanding collection of films I both can and cannot see (and that some recalcitrance goes a long way...).

Mel/Bourne/mouth, September 2017

BIBLIOGRAPHY

Amad, Paula (2010) *Counter-Archive. Film, the Everyday, and Albert Kahn's Archives de la Planète*. New York: Columbia University Press.

Delpeut, Peter (1997) *Cinéma Perdu. De eerste dertig jaar van de film 1895-1925*. Amsterdam: Uitgeverij Bas Lubberhuizen.

Friend, Tad (2016) 'The Mogul of the Middle', *The New Yorker* [Online] Available at: http://www.newyorker.com/magazine/2016/01/11/the-mogul-of-the-middle.

Grunberg, Arnon (2013) *Buster Keaton lacht nooit*. Amsterdam: Nijgh & Van Ditmar.

Jones, Janna (2012) *The Past is a Moving Picture. Preserving the Twentieth Century on Film*. Gainesville: University Press of Florida.

The Orphan in a Handbag

An introduction to the film archive and intellectual property

Op den Kamp, Claudy, *The Greatest Films Never Seen. The Film Archive and the Copyright Smokescreen.* Amsterdam University Press, 2018

DOI: 10.5117/9789462981393_INTRO

ABSTRACT

This introductory chapter explains the film archive as a research subject and describes the book's aims, its approach, and where it fits into the wider landscape of current film scholarship, concluding with an overview of its contents.

KEYWORDS
film archive, digitization, intellectual property, orphan work

This introductory chapter explains the film archive as a research subject, and describes the book's aims, its approach, and where it fits into the wider landscape of current film scholarship, concluding with an overview of its contents.

To capture the underlying idea of the book, however, we must first turn to London in 1895. Oscar Wilde's *The Importance of Being Earnest*, first staged in that year, revolves around the fortunes of a baby boy who is found in a handbag at Victoria station.[1] We learn about this incident in the opening scene, which takes place 30 years later, when the self-same orphan, Jack, asks Lady Bracknell for the hand of her only daughter, Gwendolen. We find out that an elderly gentleman, Mr. Cardew, who was mistakenly given the bag instead of his own, took the baby in, and, inspired by his own first-class train ticket to a fashionable coastal resort, bestowed on Jack the surname Worthing.

The site of the mistaken handbag incident was the station cloakroom for the Brighton line. Bewildered by Jack's revelations, Lady Bracknell declares that 'the line is immaterial'. She refuses to consider Jack's request and advises him to produce at least one parent 'before the season is quite over'. In order to marry Gwendolen, Jack is in need of both a benefactor (to provide him with social status) and acceptance into 'good society'.

Now widely seen as one of the great comedies of the English language (Cave, 2000, p. 419), *The Importance of Being Earnest* was first performed in London on St. Valentine's Day, 1895. This was one day after the Lumière brothers patented their Cinematographe,[2] a combination motion picture camera and projector, and just several months before their first public screening of projected motion pictures in Paris. Wilde could hardly have envisaged that his tale of lost parents would provide an analogy for the fate of 'orphaned films' more than 100 years later.

The term 'orphan' is applied to a copyright-protected film for which the copyright holders cannot be identified or located, rendering it unclear whose permission to seek before using the film. We will look at orphan films in more detail later, but for now it suffices to say that an orphan film's needs parallel those of Jack: a benefactor to provide it with status and fund its preservation, and acceptance into wider 'society' – that is, a place in the film-historical narrative. A film archive functions as a 'placeholder' (or 'handbag') while these needs are fulfilled. In the case of the orphan film, just as with Jack, they are interrelated: Jack must acquire social status before he can be accepted into 'society'; an orphan film needs visible status – exposure – in order to fulfil its 'potential for history making' (Jones, 2012, p. 119).

It is worth revisiting the importance of the 'Brighton line' for a moment. Victoria station is a central London terminus. This means not only that the baby could have arrived on any of the numerous lines ending at the station, but that he could also depart in any direction. And it is precisely the baby's equivocal social status that is at stake in Wilde's play. The Brighton line serviced the then-wealthy locales on Britain's southeast coast, so Jack departed from Victoria, with Mr. Cardew, in a prosperous direction – where it turns out he belonged all along. Spoiler alert: he is revealed to be Lady Bracknell's sister's son, and, by virtue of association with Lady Bracknell, he acquires the all-important social status and a place in 'good society'.[3] As a consequence, he is allowed to marry Gwendolen.

The film archive is also a sort of terminus: films can arrive from any direction, and, after a certain kind of 'place holding' in the archive, depart in others. | 19 But whether it concerns integration into high society for a man of uncertain social status at the turn of the last century, or inclusion in a wider historical narrative for an archival film with uncertain copyright ownership, the 'line', of course, is *everything*.

Knowing that a film will easily find historical recognition helps speed up the search for a benefactor. When, for instance, a 'lost' Hitchcock is found (as happened in New Zealand in 2011),[4] it is not difficult to prove its historic worth and secure funding for its restoration, moving it up the 'queue'. However, as the Preface pointed out, the films encountered in archival practice often bear little relation to the 'official' film history. What about a previously neglected, eccentric advertising film with no known copyright holder, for instance? How do you find a benefactor to fund its preservation or activate its 'potential for history making'?

The problem of the uncertain legal status of the orphan film (and its wider implications) was the catalyst for the research project that forms the basis of this book – as was the notion of the archive as a go-between or a temporary 'placeholder', where a film 'waits' until a benefactor is found and its place in film history (re)constructed.

In the last decade, the film archive's attempts to juggle the task of designing policies that allow access to its digital collections with its new responsibility of digital guardianship has brought its role as a mediator of content to the fore. The mission of a film archive, particularly a public archive, is often focused on the preservation of and the provision of access to its holdings. However, in response to the pressures of digitization and funding, these institutions feel compelled to make far-reaching decisions about whether a film will be digitized or not based on whether there is clear copyright ownership

(Hudson and Kenyon, 2007). The tension between property rights over a film as a material object and intellectual property (IP) rights over the reuse of the material (in a public-sector archive, these are usually exercized by two different parties) render the intersection of the material film archive and intellectual property a timely research subject.

This account cannot answer all of the questions raised above, but, by focusing on the human agency behind certain decisions, it attempts to unravel the 'orphan works problem' in the context of a public-sector film archive. In so doing, it reveals that this is not an exclusively legal dilemma. To date, there have been no substantial accounts of the topic, despite the challenges intellectual property presents to the provision of access to archival collections, and the repercussions this may have on our understanding of film history. This book aims to address this gap.

THE BOOK'S APPROACH

Tackling the subject of the orphan film requires an interdisciplinary vantage point. Looking at film archival collections through the lens of copyright ownership has enabled the scrutiny of discrete parts of archival collections, and has afforded the opportunity to take a meta-perspective and examine the kinds of issues that occur in categories of films as opposed to individual titles. Not only does this approach provide an insight into copyright ownership in relation to the question of access to archival collections, a previously under-explored issue, but it also allows for a close look at the consequences for another field of research, the writing of film history, which is intimately related to the intellectual property system.

In this book, we will mainly look at one of the intellectual property regimes: copyright. Copyright is a territorial notion and a national approach is taken in regards to jurisdiction. This book does not aim to provide a comprehensive overview of the international or European legal circumstances of film archives; it explores the legal status of the film material involved in digital access practices mainly in the context of Dutch law. However, restoration and access practices often involve cross-jurisdictional collaborations, so, where a transnational approach is appropriate, it visits other jurisdictions – mainly other European Union Member States and the US – in order to compare and contrast.

If legal rules are to be interpreted and understood, they need to be studied 'in context' (Twining, 2008, pp. 680-2). This study therefore adopts a contextual approach: it describes a legal phenomenon in its real-life institutional, social, and economic context, investigating how it has been influenced by that context. Its intention is not to present a bare exposition of the legal rules, but to illuminate the fact that the rules of the IP system are not and cannot be applied mechanically; rather, they are 'activated' in and by their specific context.

For a time-limited study such as this, there are distinct advantages to taking an approach that is limited to one institution. Most of the contextual conditions – institution, country, technological possibilities, and legal framework – are identical in each of the examples and remain constant throughout the investigation.

The limitation of this approach, however, is that findings in one context are not necessarily easy to map onto another – one size does not fit all. There are important divergences, for instance, between national interpretations of certain copyright regulations. Yet, although certain aspects in this book might be considered unique to the Dutch context, it provides a starting point for research in other contexts. What initially appears to be a local and exclusively legal phenomenon can also be seen in a larger context as an epistemological problem, due to its potential impact on film history. As such, this research hopes to resonate not only beyond the Netherlands, but also beyond the specific demarcation of the film archive.

Another important aspect of this book is the choice of a national public-sector film archive as the locus of the research. This is principally because this type of archive, which usually does not hold the rights to the majority of its holdings, is a prime example of where the tension between, and sometimes conflation of, rights in property and rights in intellectual property is most apparent. Again, however, other institutions, including for-profit archives, will be used for comparison where appropriate.

The various primary and secondary data sources, such as literature and archival records, are complemented with semi-structured interviews. Due to their flexibility, these interviews provide the most effective method for obtaining primary source material that is unavailable elsewhere. Interviews were conducted with staff members of a variety of institutions involved in the case studies. A set of questions was prepared but in most cases was not rigidly followed, and the length of interviews allowed for follow-up of interesting and unexpected lines of enquiry. Once completed, the interviews were transcribed to provide usable data and the transcriptions were used in a variety of ways. At some occasions, quotations have made their way directly into the text of this book. In other occasions, they have led less visibly to a particular streamlining of the consulted literature and further shaping of the research questions underpinning the book.

Overall, the book's orientation brings a fresh perspective to the subject, opening it up to a wider readership. However, before examining these topics in greater depth, we need to turn to a more detailed explanation of the film archive and its origins.

THE FILM ARCHIVE: A BRIEF HISTORY

Archival beginnings

If we take the orphan film as our starting point, including the problem of not knowing whom to ask for permission to use it, we must begin by examining in more detail how archival collections are formed. This varies along a spectrum, from legal, structured, and intentional methods through to unstructured, unintentional ways, and even blind chance. The aim of this section is not to provide a comprehensive overview of all the different ways in which collections are formed, but rather to hint at the often-haphazard fashion in which they arrive at an archive's door. The theme of archival origins will be explored in greater detail during the course of the book; it is enough to say here that obscure origins frequently lead to unpredictable destinies, as the necessary (legal) information has been lost along the way.

Many of the collections dating from the early days of film archives were accumulated in quite random ways. Initially, collectors were motivated by the 'waves of collective destruction' (Borde, 1983, p. 18) that followed each technological innovation – for example, the replacement of silent film by sound in the 1930s and the abandonment of inflammable nitrate film stock in favour of acetate in the 1950s, when it was often assumed that what came before could be either recycled for its silver content or simply discarded. It was these waves of destruction that led to the formation of the first film archives in the 1930s, and the establishment of their collective organisation, FIAF, the International Federation of Film Archives (Dupin, 2013).

In her publication, *Keepers of the Frame*, in which she traces the institutional history of the British Film Institute, Penelope Houston describes the many varied forms of film archives:

> Film archives, by their historical nature, come in all shapes, scales and sizes, have varying policies and remits, and are mostly underfunded. Many, for example, have relatively large, eclectic, international collections of which the national production represents only a proportion of the whole; some others concentrate more, in varying degrees, on caring for the films of their own country. A few have systems of legal deposit which guarantee (for recent years, at least) a higher rate of deposit of national productions. But most do not. (Houston, 1994, p. 165)

Film archives not only differ in origin and size, however, but also in organisational structure and funding: they can be funded publicly, privately, or through a combination of both (Fossati, 2009). Some of these organisational structures have direct consequences for the composition of the collections: for instance, the holdings of most public archives can be characterized by their national or regional focus, whereas the holdings of most privately held archives appear to reflect their copyright ownership.

Houston describes the early decades of film archiving as the collection of 'material of uncertain provenance, as well as films picked up from private collectors or from outside the system of heavily policed industry control' (1994, p. 3). It was often considered best to remain secretive about holdings to avoid attracting the attention of rights holders.

Archival collections are also built up by 'chance elements, such as grants, discoveries or acquisitions' (de Kuyper, 2013, p. 127). Some parts of archival holdings are accumulated more or less randomly; these holdings often start out as 'stuff' that has turned up at the archive's door, which can make for a quite heterogeneous collection. Generally, a film archive's collection does not exclusively consist of films; it often includes non-film material. The archive might collect, for example, projectors, posters, film stills, filmmakers' paper archives, or even film props and cinema décor. The part of the collection that does consist of films will not exclusively carry complete titles, but multiple versions of the same title, scene outtakes, unedited camera negatives, incomplete films, and even film fragments, some of which are unidentified. The holdings often comprise innumerable types of different formats, only some of which have become industry-wide standards; others will no longer be playable. It is hardly surprising that, in many of these cases, it is not clear who made what or who owns what anymore.

Over the course of the latter half of the 20th century, the archiving field was subject to a certain amount of professionalization, and this has been reflected in a shift in the foundational body of literature. Where it initially focused on portraits of individual institutions and the myriad eccentric figures who spearheaded them (Roud, 1983; Houston, 1994), this body of work has recently been supplemented by specialized texts, which address the field more comprehensively, attempting to define such concepts as 'patrimony' and (cultural) 'heritage' (Fossati, 2009; Frick, 2011).

This professionalization has also been recognized on a national scale, and some countries – for example, Denmark, Finland, France, and Poland – have adopted a mandatory legal deposit system (Gorini, 2004). In most cases, this means that a national archive is designated to hold copies of all audiovisual works that have received government funding, in an attempt to establish a national cultural patrimony. Although other countries such as the Netherlands do not adhere to such a deposit system, an archive's decisions on selection, acquisition, and exchange will also shape its collection in fundamental ways. Equally, its strategies for preservation and access will help shape the wider film-historical narrative – for instance, as the senior curator of EYE, Mark-Paul Meyer, points out (2011), the reevaluation of colour in early cinema was influenced by new restoration techniques.

What these examples reveal is the dichotomy between the canonical text-book film histories and the actual material holdings of a film archive. The archive is not a place where pristine copies of complete films lie dormant, simply waiting to be 'roused' to life (Amad, 2010, p. 159); more often than not, it is a place where the marginal is the norm and a significant portion of the material is in a fragmentary state (Delpeut, 1990).

Furthermore, in the analogue era, two categories of the archive's work were 'at odds with each other [...]: preservation and access' (de Kuyper, 2013, p. 122). These two archival missions sometimes appeared to conflict so utterly that some archives took the radical decision to focus exclusively on one to the detriment of the other. The early curators of the National Film Archive (UK) and the Cinémathèque française, Ernest Lindgren and Henri Langlois, respectively, were classic embodiments of this tension. Lindgren personified the idea of preservation for the sake of posterity in its most polemical form, allowing no provision for access; Langlois, a collector at heart, was dedicated to screening films, regardless of the need for preservation (Houston, 1994, pp. 44–49).

A key change in the last decade, however, has been the shift to a digital culture, partially driven by funding imperatives. The funding for preservation is often linked to an obligation to provide archival access, which in turn appears to be synonymous with digital and online access (Cherchi Usai, 2009). Whereas archival access in previous decades meant screening programmes, museum exhibitions, and on-site study, there is now an 'expectation not merely from the public but also from their political representatives that the collections of publicly funded institutions will be accessible to view and to study online' (Padfield, 2010, p. 208).[5] As a consequence, preservation and access are now seen as two sides of the same coin (Nissen, 2002).

Digitization

It is clear that new technologies and distribution techniques are creating novel ways to access and use collections. Digitization in particular has and will continue to have far-reaching implications for the way in which film works can be preserved, exploited, and protected.

Over the last decade, discussions about digitization in relation to the collections of cultural heritage institutions have gathered steam. For many archives, however, the dream of a full digital facsimile of their holdings is a world away, despite the fact that the digital age appears to offer 'seemingly guarantee[d] instant accessibility' (Horak, 2007, p. 29). Indeed, Kristin Thompson argues that the so-called celestial multiplex, in which every film is available at any time for free at the click of a mouse, will not appear any time soon. Although her article was published in 2007, Thompson's rationale still holds true.

There are innumerable discussions about the potential costs of digitization and the loss of information when scanning films (as well as the virtue of continuing to screen film as film), the long-term digital preservation and storage battles, and whether digitization spells the end of film. However, the inevitable digital change has already occurred in the archival practices of distribution and access. And archives find themselves in a bind:

> Although large-scale digitization projects of film collections have been extensively discussed in the last ten years by many archives and some of them are ongoing, archivists are still struggling with the questions regarding the kind of access that should be granted to their users once the content would be available in digital form. In other words, the question is whether film archives will move on from the chaperone model and let go of their collections, acknowledging the new role of the users. (Fossati, 2009, p. 97)

But 'letting go' of collections, allowing users to explore these new digital archives on their own without a 'chaperone', does not mean that the traditional role of the archivist as a human gatekeeper – a role closely associated with the analogue archive – has disappeared. These new archives may be performative, but the archivists are still the 'editors of knowledge' (Noordegraaf, 2010). Indeed, the element of human agency can be discerned clearly in the process of digitization: the works that are most frequently made public are the ones that are easiest to digitize – that is, works that (aside from restoration issues) have a secure legal provenance (Hudson and Kenyon, 2007), and someone has to make that decision.

Consider, for instance, the now defunct Dutch initiative, 'Ximon'. Developed in light of the national digitization project, 'Images for the Future', one of the reasons behind the creation of this video-on-demand platform was to avoid the problem of the material's legal status dominating the character of the portal. However, in practice, the decision of what to present online was mainly determined by 'what was clearable' (Rechsteiner, 2010), a process that is highly dependable on human negotiation skills.

Thus, the 'challenge of digital reproduction' has meant that 'intellectual property has come to be a household term' (David and Halbert, 2014, p. xlix). Issues of digitization and copyright are intertwined in the film archive because widely held assumptions about the nature of film itself owe their provenance not only to what evidence is kept in the archives but, more importantly, on how much of that evidence is publicly accessible, which is a theme throughout this book.

Although this book's primary site of investigation is the film archive, it is focused more specifically on the archive's digital access practices, as the impact of copyright is most palpable in the area in which the archive intersects with the outside world. It is only through access to films that we can construct frameworks of meaning and start to fathom the implications of digitization and intellectual property for the understanding of film history. (In the context of this book, film history will mean the kind of film history that focuses on extant film material, as not all kinds of film history are written based on archival material nor are they all written within the context of the film archive, a theme we will return to later in the book.)

Intellectual property

Aside from the primary dichotomy between the canonical film histories we find in textbooks and the actual material holdings of a film archive, a second can be discerned: the copyright dichotomy between intellectual and material property. Film archives own or hold on deposit many physical works of film; the copyright owner, on the other hand, might be someone quite different: 'The ownership of the copyright is independent of the ownership of the physical medium in which the work is expressed, and so it is perfectly possible for one person to own copyright in an object physically owned by another' (Hunter, 2012, p. 41).

The distinction between intellectual and material property is particularly interesting in the context of public-sector institutions. These institutions own or hold on deposit numerous material holdings but hold the copyright to almost none; meanwhile, they often have a remit to preserve and provide access to their holdings. The balance between ownership and the exchange of ideas is key to the debates over intellectual property (David and Halbert, 2014). This tension is a theme that will be explored throughout the course of the book.

Film is a fragile material that needs special preservation treatment, and film archives often have to duplicate original elements in order to ensure the long-term survival of their contents. Duplicating works and communicating them to the public are considered to be copyright-restricted activities and the consent of the rights holder is needed.

As early as 1991, the UNITED NATIONS EDUCATIONAL SCIENTIFIC AND

CULTURAL ORGANIZATION (UNESCO) produced a report, *Legal Questions Facing Audiovisual Archives*, in response to the desire of the UNESCO Consultation of Experts on the Development of Audiovisual Archives in 1984 to 'initiate a study of copyright in relation to moving images to determine the changes necessary to permit moving image archives to function, and a parallel study of archival legislation to determine how archives can be exempted from copyright restrictions' (p. 3). The report concluded that there were indeed international conventions and recommendations that related to audiovisual *material*, but they did not in any way relate to audiovisual *archives*. There was little recognition of the special position of archives as keepers of the audiovisual heritage and no recommendations had been integrated into national copyright legislation.

More recently, institutions in the GLAM sector (galleries, libraries, archives, and museums) in many countries have been able to rely on a preservation exception in certain circumstances, which means they are allowed to reproduce work without the rights owner's permission if the aim is to protect the work from decay or to keep it accessible if the technology through which it is accessed has become obsolete. In the Netherlands, for instance, this preservation exception has been in place for some time, although in the UK, format shifting was considered a breach of copyright until recent changes in the law accommodated this exception.[6]

Initially, although the literature that addressed copyright in the context of film archives, or cultural heritage more generally, emanated from the legal as well as the archival field, it never strayed beyond its own disciplinary boundaries. More recently, however, we have started to see a sort of cross-fertilization as each field begins to address the implications of one area for the other. One of the earliest cross-fertilization studies was undertaken in the light of copyright clearance for archival footage in the realm of documentary film. The authors clearly showed that the avoidance of clearance problems 'may dictate filmmakers' choices of subject-matter, influencing them, for example, to avoid projects involving current events or modern history – which tend to be minefields [...] because strict compliance through licensing is often required' (Aufderheide and Jaszi, 2004, p. 29).

The literature, particularly the legal literature, dealing with one of the main topics in the field of copyright in the context of the film archive – orphan works – initially stalled at the notion that collections remained dormant as a consequence of rights issues, as it was concerned with mapping the orphan works problem, including its causes and potential solutions (USCO, 2006; van Gompel, 2007a; 2007b; Elferink and Ringnalda, 2008; van Gompel and Hugenholtz, 2010; JISC, 2011; Pallante, 2012a; 2012b; Borghi and Karapapa, 2013; Favale et al., 2013).

As a result of (predominantly) EU-funded research projects and initiatives, archival practice has mostly contributed to this debate in the form of project deliverables. In the context of the EU project, European Film Gateway, for instance, it has led to such texts as the *Report on Legal Frameworks in European Film Gateway (efg) Consortium Member States* (2009) and the *Final Guidelines on Copyright Clearance and IPR Management* (2010). Mainly focused on laying out the current legislation in several EU member states, these studies did not deal with any of the implications of potential restrictions to archival access.

Legal restrictions have such a profound influence on what the film-historical field takes as its objects of study, it is surprising that only a handful of media scholars have addressed copyright issues more generally in the larger cultural and creative industries' context. Thompson (2007), in her aforementioned article on the 'celestial multiplex', identifies copyright issues as one of the main factors why she believes such a phenomenon will not materialize any time soon. Lucas Hilderbrand, in *Inherent Vice* (2009), analyses the specific case study of analogue VHS tape and its ties to bootlegging and preservation practices, while raising issues of intellectual property rights. Peter Decherney, in *Hollywood's Copyright Wars* (2012), as well as in some of his other writings, illustrates how the Hollywood studios and intellectual property laws have shaped each other reciprocally. However, it is only very recently that the potential effect of the unavailability of heritage materials – caused by diverse copyright issues – on preserving, accessing, and understanding digital cultural heritage has made its way into the literature from a legal point of view (McCausland, 2009; Derclaye, 2010; Wallace, 2016; Deazley, 2017).

A firmer bridge needs to be erected between these still relatively discrete bodies of literature by addressing the broader question of how and why only a part of extant archival material is publicly accessible, and the repercussions of this for our wider cultural understanding. The following chapters take up this task.

STRUCTURE OF THE BOOK

The primary purpose of this study is to examine the relationship between the film archive, copyright, and film material's potential for 'history making' based on how much of the material is publicly accessible. The next chapter (Chapter 1) introduces a specific public-sector national film archive, and explains why it plays such a central role in the book.

The following three chapters draw a picture of a 'recategorized' film archive based on the copyright ownership of the material. This helps to unravel the practices that govern access to the archived films according to discrete legal categories. Each chapter looks at a result of this recategorization, discussed in Chapter 1, including the *embargoed film* (Chapter 2), the *orphan film* (Chapter 3), and the *public-domain film* (Chapter 4).

Bringing together the preceding three chapters, Chapter 5 focuses on the practice of found-footage filmmaking as a specific artistic intervention in the reuse of film in the institutional context of the archive. Chapter 6 then takes a step back to examine copyright practices and the production of film history in the archival context, focusing on a particular historical example.

Finally, the last chapter draws some conclusions about the relationship between the film archive and copyright based on the discussion in the preceding chapters, as well as addressing the specific combination of the legal context and human agency in an institutional setting – a discussion that is threaded throughout the book.

NOTES

1   My thanks go to Michael Punt for pointing me in the direction of this material.
2   The full patent text in French is available at: http://cinematographes.free.fr/ lumiere-245032.html (accessed on 17 March 2018).
3   Lady Bracknell, in turn, has rewritten her own story, as she had no fortune of any kind when she married and has done a significant amount of social climbing since then (Cave, 2000).
4   See, for instance, https://www.theguardian.com/film/2011/aug/03/alfred-hitchcock-film-new-zealand (accessed on 7 September 2017).
5   This mainly pertains to national archives in Europe; it is, for instance, not a categorical imperative for American nonprofit archives.
6   See Chapter 8 of 'Copyright 101', Copyright and Digital Cultural Heritage: Exceptions for Libraries, Archives and Museums, at the online resource, the Copyright Cortex. Available at: https://copyrightcortex.org/ (accessed on 25 September 2017).

BIBLIOGRAPHY

Amad, Paula (2010) *Counter-Archive. Film, the Everyday, and Albert Kahn's Archives de la Planète*. New York: Columbia University Press.

Aufderheide, Patricia and Peter Jaszi (2004) *Untold Stories: Creative Consequences of the Rights Clearance Culture for Documentary Filmmakers*. Washington, DC: Center for Social Media, American University.

Borde, Raymond (1983) *Les Cinémathèques*. Lausanne: Editions L'Age d'Homme.

Borghi, Maurizio, and Stavroula Karapapa (2013) *Copyright and Mass Digitization. A Cross-Jurisdictional Perspective*. Oxford: Oxford University Press.

Cave, Richard Allen (ed.) (2000) *The Importance of Being Earnest, and Other Plays*. London: Penguin Classics.

Cherchi Usai, Paolo (2009) 'Are All (Analog) Films "Orphans"? A Pre-digital Appraisal', *The Moving Image*, 9(1), pp. 1–18.

David, Matthew, and Debora Halbert (eds.) (2014) *The SAGE Handbook of Intellectual Property*. London: SAGE Publications Ltd.

Deazley, Ronan (2017) 'Copyright 101', *Copyright Cortex* [online] available at: https://copyrightcortex.org/copyright-101 (accessed on 25 September 2017).

Decherney, Peter (2012) *Hollywood Copyright Wars*. New York: Columbia University Press.

de Kuyper, Eric de (2013) 'Werken bij een Filmarchief/Filmmuseum, of: Schizofrenie als opdracht', in: Cinemathèque royale de Belgique (ed.) *75000 Films*. Crisnée: Editions Yellow Now, pp. 121–137.

Delpeut, Peter (1990) 'BITS & PIECES - De grenzen van het filmarchief', *Versus*, 2, pp. 75–84.

Derclaye, Estelle (ed.) (2010) *Copyright and Cultural Heritage. Preservation and Access to Works in a Digital World*. Cheltenham: Edward Elgar Publishing.

Dupin, Christophe (2013) 'First Tango in Paris: The Birth of FIAF, 1936-1938', *The Journal of Film Preservation*, 88, pp. 43–57.

Elferink, Mirjam and Allard Ringnalda (2008) *Digitale Ontsluiting van Historische Archieven en Verweesde Werken: Een Inventarisatie*. Utrecht: CIER [Online]. Available at: http://www.wodc.nl/onderzoeksdatabase/ontsluiting-historische-archieven-en-auteursrecht-hoe-beter.aspx?cp=44&cs=6796 (accessed on 21 April 2016).

EFG (2009) *Report on legal frameworks in European Film Gateway (EFG) consortium member states*. Amsterdam: European Film Gateway [Online]. Available at: http://www.edfgproject.eu/downloads/D.5.1_legal_frameworks_in_EFG_consortium_a.pdf (accessed on 21 April 2016).

EFG (2010) *Final Guidelines on Copyright Clearance and IPR Management*. Amsterdam: European Film Gateway [Online]. Available at: pro.europeana.eu/documents/.../EFG_D5.3_Copyright_Clearance.pdf (accessed on 4 November 2010).

Favale, Marcella, Fabian Homberg, Martin Kretschmer, Dinusha Mendis, and Davide Secchi (2013) *Copyright, and the Regulation of Orphan Works: A comparative review of seven jurisdictions and a rights clearance simulation*. CREATe working paper. Available at: http://www.create.ac.uk/publications/copyright-and-the-regulation-of-orphan-works/ (accessed on 11 October 2017).

Fossati, Giovanna (2009) *From Grain to Pixel: The Archival Life of Film in Transition*. Amsterdam: Amsterdam University Press.

Frick, Caroline (2011) *Saving Cinema. The Politics of Preservation.* New York: Oxford University Press.

Gorini, Sabina (2004) 'The Protection of Cinematographic Heritage in Europe'. *IRIS Plus, a supplement to IRIS, Legal Observations of the European Audiovisual Observatory*, 08, pp. 1–8.

Hilderbrand, Lucas (2009) *Inherent Vice: Bootleg Histories of Videotape and Copyright.* Durham: Duke University Press.

Horak, Jan-Christopher (2007) 'The Gap Between 1 and 0: Digital Video and the Omissions of Film History', *Spectator*, 27(1), pp. 29–41.

Houston, Penelope (1994) *Keepers of the Frame: The Film Archives.* London: British Film Institute.

Hudson, Emily, and Andrew Kenyon (2007) 'Digital Access: The Impact of Copyright in Digitisation Practices in Australian Museums, Galleries, Libraries and Archives', *UNSW Law Journal*, 30(1), pp. 12–52.

Hunter, Dan (2012) *The Oxford Introductions to U.S. Law: Intellectual Property.* New York: Oxford University Press.

JISC (2009) *In From the Cold: An Assessment of the Scope of 'Orphan Works' and Its Impact on the Delivery of Services to the Public.* Strategic Content Alliance, Collections Trust [Online]. Available at: http://www.jisc.ac.uk/publications/reports/2009/infromthecold.aspx (accessed on 21 April 2016).

Jones, Janna (2012) *The Past is a Moving Picture. Preserving the Twentieth Century on Film.* Gainesville: University Press of Florida.

McCausland, Sally (2009) 'Getting Public Broadcaster Archives Online', *Media and Arts Law Review*, 14(2), pp. 142–165.

Meyer, Mark-Paul (2011) 'Authenticiteit en fotografische materialiteit', in Annemieke de Jong (ed.) *Zorgen voor onzichtbare assets. Over het behoud van digitale AV-collecties.* Hilversum: Beeld en Geluid, pp. 95–108.

Nissen, Dan (ed.) (2002) *Preserve Then Show.* Copenhagen: Danish Film Institute.

Noordegraaf, Julia (2010) 'Performing the Archive: Archivists as Editors of Knowledge', *Reimagining the Archive: Remapping and Remixing Traditional Models in the Digital Age*, UCLA, Los Angeles, 12–14 November.

Padfield, Tim (2010) 'Preserving and Accessing our Cultural Heritage – Issues for Cultural Sector Institutions: Archives, Libraries, Museums and Galleries', in Estelle Derclaye (ed.) *Copyright and Cultural Heritage. Preservation and Access to Works in a Digital World.* Cheltenham: Edward Elgar Publishing, pp. 195–209.

Pallante, Maria (2012a) 'Orphan Works & Mass Digitization: Obstacles & Opportunities' [Keynote Address] *Berkeley Digital Copyright Project*, Berkeley Center for Law and Technology, 12 April 2012.

Pallante, Maria (2012b) 'Orphan Works and Mass Digitization', *Federal Register*, 77(204), Washington, DC: Library of Congress, Copyright Office, pp. 64555–64561.

Rechsteiner, Emjay (Curator Contemporary Dutch Film, Eye Film Institute Nether-
  lands)(2010) Interviewed by Claudy Op den Kamp. Philadelphia, US, 6 November.
Roud, Richard (1983) *A Passion for Films: Henri Langlois and the Cinémathèque
  Française*. New York: The Viking Press.
Thompson, Kristin (2007) 'The Celestial Multiplex', *Observations on Film Art* [Online].
  Available at: http://www.davidbordwell.net/blog/2007/03/27/the-celestial-
  multiplex/ (accessed on 21 April 2016).
Twining, William (2008) 'Law in Context Movement', in Peter Cane and Joanne
  Conaghan (eds.) *The New Oxford Companion to Law*. Oxford: Oxford University
  Press.
UNITED NATIONS EDUCATIONAL SCIENTIFIC AND CULTURAL ORGANIZATION (UNESCO)
  (1991) *Legal Questions Facing Audiovisual Archives*. Paris: UNESCO [Online]. Avail-
  able at: unesdoc.unesco.org/images/0008/000886/088674e.pdf (accessed on 21
  April 2016).
United States Copyright Office (USCO) (2006) *Report on Orphan Works*. Washington:
  Library of Congress.
van Gompel, Stef van (2007a) 'Audiovisual Archives and the Inability to Clear Rights in
  Orphan Works', *IRIS Plus, a supplement to IRIS, Legal Observations of the European
  Audiovisual Observatory*, 04, pp. 1–8.
van Gompel, Stef van (2007b) 'Unlocking the Potential of Pre-Existing Content: How to
  Address the Issue of Orphan Works in Europe?', *IIC*, 6/2007, pp. 669-702.
van Gompel, Stef, and Bernt Hugenholtz (2010) 'The Orphan Works Problem: The
  Copyright Conundrum of Digitizing Large-Scale Audiovisual Archives, and How to
  Solve It', *Popular Communication. The International Journal of Media and Culture*,
  8(1), pp. 61–71.
Wallace, Andrea (2016) 'Cultural Institutions and Surrogate Intellectual Property
  Rights: Resisting an Artwork's Transfer into the Public Domain', *ISHTIP confe-
  rence*, University of Glasgow, 6–8 July.

ABOUT THE AUTHOR

Claudy Op den Kamp is Lecturer in Film and faculty member at the Centre for Intellectual Property Policy and Management at Bournemouth University, UK, and Adjunct
Research Fellow at Swinburne Law School, Australia.

CHAPTER 1

Terra Incognita
The Nederlands Filmmuseum / EYE Film Institute Netherlands

Op den Kamp, Claudy, *The Greatest Films Never Seen. The Film Archive and the Copyright Smokescreen.* Amsterdam University Press, 2018

DOI: 10.5117/9789462981393_CH01

ABSTRACT

This chapter looks in detail at the rationale behind the book's focus on the EYE Film Institute Netherlands and introduces a recategorization of the archival film collection based on copyright ownership. The resulting categories (the embargoed film, the orphan film, and the public domain film) will function as the basis for an analysis of digital archival access practices in the following chapters.

KEYWORDS
Nederlands Filmmuseum, EYE Film Institute, historical resonance, recategorization

Villa Koningshof in Overveen
(courtesy of EYE Film Institute)

'The only true voyage of discovery, would be not to visit strange lands but to possess other eyes'
(Marcel Proust, *À la recherche du temps perdu*)

This chapter looks in more detail at the rationale behind the book's focus on the EYE Film Institute Netherlands (known simply as EYE) and explores how the two dichotomies mentioned in the Introduction play out in practice in this particular national film archive.

The first dichotomy is between canonical 'textbook' film histories and the material holdings in a film archive. Chance, as well as choice, has played a role in the formation of EYE's collection. This chapter looks at how the institute's adoption of a distinctive aesthetic attitude towards preservation led to the opening up of its archive and endowed its noncanonical archival holdings with historical resonance. In the process, it created a potentially rich primary source for film-historical research, and encouraged the growth of interest (and expertise) in the artistic practice of found-footage filmmaking.

The chapter also places a second dichotomy, between the intellectual and material ownership of works, under scrutiny. It introduces a recategorization of the archival film collection based on copyright ownership. The resulting categories (the embargoed film, the orphan film, and the public domain film) will function as the basis for an analysis of digital archival access practices in the following chapters.

WHAT'S IN A NAME?

EYE – the film sector's institute of Dutch cinema and national museum of film – is the result of a merger in 2010 of four institutions,[1] including the former Nederlands Filmmuseum. This account uses both names, the Nederlands Filmmuseum and EYE, to highlight the precise timing of the events under discussion: Nederlands Filmmuseum is used when discussing events taking place before 2010; EYE is used after that date, and whenever the institute is mentioned more generally.

EYE is one of two national audiovisual archives in the Netherlands. The other, the largest in the country, is the archive of the national broadcasting corporations – the Netherlands Institute for Sound and Vision. The Netherlands also has several regional archives, some of whose collections are exclusively composed of audiovisual material.

EYE is not the only institution that displays the tensions inherent in the two dichotomies mentioned above; they can also be seen in the practices of the Netherlands Institute for Sound and Vision, and in many other not-for-profit cultural institutions. However, its digital access practices present a slightly more apposite context for this analysis. The institute is not only focused on collecting, preserving, and restoring its collections; as it is partly subsidized by public money (Fossati, 2009) and is a not-for-profit institution – like all the national archives belonging to the International Federation of Film Archives (FIAF) – EYE is also mandated to provide access to its holdings. However, it holds the rights to only a very small proportion of its collection (the estimate is less than 5%, a similar number to the British Film Institute),[2] and this means that some of the steps it needs to take towards providing access are restrained by copyright. A further important characteristic is the fact that it often collaborates in cross-jurisdictional restoration projects, due to the international character of film preservation, which relies on the exchange of film elements and international (online) distribution.

Also, over the last four decades or so, EYE has taken an active stance when it comes to the creation of historical resonance for its own collection by reflecting on its historiographic position and challenging that of other archives. It has accomplished this through, for example, engaging in found-footage filmmaking practices – that is, 'writing history with the films themselves' (Fossati, 2012, p. 179); it has not only collected filmmakers' work for its permanent collection, but has also invited artists into the institute to work with the archival films, a theme we will return to in Chapter 5.

As one of this book's concerns is the concept of the archive as a storehouse of films that are potential sources of film history, its periodization roughly comprises the last 40 years of film archiving. This not only corresponds with the practices described above, but also with the birth of an understanding of films and archives as primary historical sources and a realization of the changing nature of filmic evidence and the importance of films previously perceived as marginal. This timeframe hinges on the landmark 1978 FIAF Congress, held in Brighton in the UK, which is commonly regarded as a turning point in film historiography. Indeed, the Brighton Congress and the changes in archival practice could be seen as interrelated. The Congress itself will be explored in more detail in Chapter 6 as part of a larger historical contextualization of the 'return' to archival film as a primary source.

DICHOTOMY I: CREATING HISTORICAL RESONANCE

EYE has been instrumental in the rewriting of film history based on the material it has made available over the last few decades. Giovanna Fossati notes:

> [D]eputy directors Eric de Kuyper first, and Peter Delpeut later, encouraged restoration and presentation practices that were mainly moved by the aesthetic value of films rather than by their historical relevance. [...] From this perspective, the focus shifted from the celebrated centerpieces of official film history to its margins. (Fossati, 2009, p. 172)

As part of the 'return' to archival film evidence in the late 1980s and early 1990s, the Nederlands Filmmuseum focused on (the aesthetics of) the films in its own collection rather than the accepted canonical titles. As the films themselves were brought to light, viewed, and examined, the whole concept of the film archive changed: it was no longer regarded as *terra incognita*, uncharted territory, but as a potentially vital primary source for written film history. By revealing the fragmented nature of its collection of surviving films, the institute helped establish the historical resonance of its holdings, thus challenging the traditional canon.

During the first 40 years of its existence, the Nederlands Filmmuseum concentrated predominantly on collecting. The senior curator of EYE, Mark-Paul Meyer, reflects on the collection's beginnings:

> Just as many other film museums, the Filmmuseum in Amsterdam was started up shortly after World War II by enthusiastic cinephiles who were interested in collecting films to ensure that they would not be lost. While the Filmmuseum's archive expanded over the following decennia through contributions from collectors, the largest part of the collection was donated by distributors, filmmakers and producers. Due to this, the archive was a reflection of the film climate in the Netherlands, and by definition, it was characterized by both chance and lacunae. (Meyer, 2012, p. 146)

The museum, however, was far from being a focused and well-organized institution: its collecting practices were shaped by its limited budget, and the items themselves were 'piled up in the basement in a cluttered chaos' (Delpeut, 1998, p. 2). But when Hoos Blotkamp (previously head of visual arts and architecture at the Ministry of Welfare, Public Health, and Culture) became its director in 1987, the Nederlands Filmmuseum was 'awoken by a kiss' (Hendriks, 1996, p. 109). In 1988, Blotkamp appointed filmmaker and scholar Eric de Kuyper as its first deputy director, and it was de Kuyper who was responsible for the huge increase in the number of screenings. Just a few years later, the museum secured a substantial grant to tackle the backlog in its nitrate preservation (Hendriks, 1996).[3] In order to deal with what she termed a 'conglomerate of broom closets' (Hendriks, 1996, p. 109), Blotkamp took a pragmatic attitude towards archiving, which could be described as 'start at the bottom right and end at the top left' (Delpeut, 1998, p. 2). This meant that, in a very post-Brighton spirit,[4] everything was taken out of the archive and viewed from a fresh perspective.

This in itself was a revolutionary move: it was not standard practice to view a film before deciding on its preservation. In similar institutions in other countries, such as the Cinémathèque française, such decisions were often made by external committees after consulting a list of films, a practice guaranteed to maintain the dominance of the established canon (Delpeut, 2012). De Kuyper (1994, p. 102) criticized this approach, which he claimed meant that archives adopted a 'common approach to the history of film' as opposed to letting their discrete programmes 'reflect the collections' or 'reflect on film history'.

Blotkamp and de Kuyper took a very different approach at the Nederlands Filmmuseum: they relied on the expertise of staff members, who were asked to view the films and then make a decision on what to preserve based on their own tastes and personal insights. This encouraged unique, sometimes inspired choices (Delpeut, 1998). The film prints themselves became the point of departure (Hertogs and de Klerk, 1994). Meyer emphasizes how the composition of the collection itself was fundamental to the Filmmuseum's innovative preservation and presentation methods:

> To a large extent, the archive was only accessible in a limited way at the end of the 1980s. While the films were properly registered, much about the films was still a mystery; identification, technical quality, and the determination of the cinematographic importance left much to be desired. In fact, there was only one way to change the situation: to take everything out of the vault, film can by film can, and see what each contained. It turned out that there was much to discover and, in the process of going through everything, it became clear that what was in the film history books didn't match with what the Filmmuseum had in its vaults. There were titles from well-known directors, of course, but by far the majority of what was discovered was completely unknown material – often masterful or exceptionally beautiful work that deserved a place in film history – or film history as the Filmmuseum would propagate it. (Meyer, 2012, p. 146)

This practice of viewing the material before reaching a decision on its preservation, letting chance play a role, led to an eclectic film collection. EYE's collection bears little resemblance to those of other archives, as most of the material uncovered in those early days turned out to be unknown, 'wonderful rubbish' (Meyer, in Olesen, 2013), and 'scarcely traceable to the canon of cinema history' (Delpeut, 2012, p. 220). Mainly as a result of decay and lost material, a significant number of films turned out to be incomplete. These fragmentary films became an analogy for the incomplete nature of the film archive and of film history itself (Lameris, 2017). De Kuyper (1991, p. 10) addresses the general denial of the archive's incompleteness in an article in which he speaks of 'falsifying' and 'distorting film history' by not taking archival lacunae into consideration. Blotkamp, in turn, believed that it was essential to bring the curious and neglected parts of film history to the attention of the public as '[o]thers had set foot on the beaten paths of history sufficiently already' (Delpeut, 1998, p. 4).

The fundamental building blocks of a new Dutch preservation policy therefore rested on three factors. The first was the specific composition of the Filmmuseum's archive, which comprised a high number of noncanonical titles. The museum's own collection took centre stage because it was regarded as a direct reflection of film culture in the Netherlands. The second factor was the emergence of a particular historiographic position, which claimed that film history necessarily presents an incomplete image; there is no *one* film history, but several. And the third was the existence of what was thought of as a specifically 'Dutch' attitude towards preservation – that is, since one of the archive's tasks was to present and reflect on film history, it was essential to address its discrepancies and lacunae.

The composition of EYE's collection, its public mission, and its specific attitude form a coherent theme that runs throughout the book – one that is arguably still reflected in EYE's practices today. For example, in response to the opening at EYE of the Orphan Film Symposium in March 2014, Peter Delpeut remarked that 'technical knowledge, fortitude of content and above all creative forms of presentation still characterize the work of the current staff'.[5] This includes inviting artists to reuse its holdings creatively, as well as finding novel ways of presenting its collection. This attitude – with its emphasis on human agency – will be a significant factor when we turn to analyzing access to specific film categories in the next chapters.

The new preservation policy at the Nederlands Filmmuseum was part of a wider post-Brighton shift from the 'old' to the 'new' film history that took place in both the academic and archival worlds. The aim was to place previously unknown films in the spotlight (Lameris, 2017). This unique development, however, did not in itself create a collection that was ready to be programmed

– the many unknown films and film fragments were in need of contextualization. EYE's current head of collection, Frank Roumen, who began his career at
the Nederlands Filmmuseum in 1988, comments:

> We had this insight that we should move to what we had in the archive,
> what we owned, and search for ways and forms of presenting [...] short,
> silent, and unknown films. [...] [W]e started to experiment with [the addi-
> tion of] theatrical [aspects], live music, orchestra[s], and compilations.
> (Roumen, cited in Escareño, 2009, p. 190)

De Kuyper and Delpeut, who both played an instrumental role in the international film archival practice of the late 1980s and early 1990s, provided a
context for the collection of the Nederlands Filmmuseum. Both addressed the
discrepancy between archival films relegated to obscurity and canonical film
history on several occasions. Delpeut, for instance, advocated that the archive | 41
be seen as an 'aesthetic repository', which would in turn provide the source
material for the Filmmuseum's programming:

> The films should firstly be the subject of pleasure and should only be sec-
> ondarily the subject of identification (and all related rational activities).
> That state of affairs can provoke the film archive to approach film history
> [...] more from an aesthetic standpoint than from a historical one. Films
> exist then as the bearer of an affective relationship, not merely as a histori-
> cal fact. This also means that when screening the films from the archive
> they should firstly be presented as fun and entertaining facts, not as his-
> torical facts. Perhaps this would also provoke a different kind of choices,
> other selections in conservation schemes. (Delpeut, 1990, pp. 83-84)

Together, de Kuyper and Delpeut took the focus on the aesthetic rather than
the historic aspect of moving images to the extreme by reanimating hidden,
forgotten, and fragmented film history. They placed unknown material centre
stage by preserving, presenting, and disseminating unidentified fragments.
For example, the BITS & PIECES collection at the Nederlands Filmmuseum,
established in the late 1980s and early 1990s, is a 'series of (generally) short
unidentified fragments of film, preserved primarily on account of the aesthetic value of the images' (Hertogs and de Klerk, 1994, p. 9).[6] At the heart of this
policy of preserving and presenting the unidentified and neglected fragments
lay the desire to challenge the prevailing historiographic orthodoxy:

> The reason why they are neglected is that they do not have, and can't be
> given, a label. They are not registered and cannot be part of traditional

film history. We don't have criteria to select them. [...] The result is that a film, which cannot be labelled with the help of the notions mentioned, cannot acquire a historical identity. That means, literally, it does not exist for film history. (de Kuyper, 1994, pp. 104–105)

These unidentified fragments will be explored in more detail as orphan works in Chapter 3 and as raw ingredients for new films in Chapter 5.

The need for contextualization in this new preservation policy went hand in hand with the demand for academic reflection. The institute organized numerous academic symposia to answer these needs. The International Amsterdam Workshop, in particular, was arguably an heir to the Brighton Congress – this series of workshops allowed an international peer group of film scholars, film archivists, and relevant experts to watch and discuss materials and topics that had previously been under-researched in both the film historiographical and film archival fields (Hertogs and de Klerk, 1994; 1996).[7]

More recently, EYE launched an imprint with Amsterdam University Press, entitled 'Framing Film', a series of scholarly works 'dedicated to theoretical and analytical studies in restoration, collection, archival, and exhibition practices in line with the existing archive of EYE'.[8] Aside from this book, Fossati's 2009 publication, *From Grain to Pixel*, which charts the changing preservation and restoration practices of a film archive in transition from the analogue to the digital era, and Bregt Lameris' 2017 publication, *Film Museum Practice and Film Historiography*, on the interaction between film preservation practices and film-historical discourses, are works that are published within the imprint, and which both also centre on EYE.[9] These works contribute to the argument that, in the context of the archival institution, historiography does not mean a mere succession of epistemic shifts; rather, the archive contains multiple film-historical attitudes. The processes of collecting, restoring, and presenting all reflect 'some ideology, however unconscious, associated with a certain historical taste' (de Kuyper, in Hertogs and de Klerk, 1996, p. 79). In film restoration, for instance, ideas about which elements should be reproduced are subject to continuous change:

Film restorers are, in fact, creative film historians who render interpretations of film history visible: they create new versions of the archival films, which reveal the dominant film historical perspective at the time of restoration. (Lameris, 2017, p. 122)

EYE understands that the archivist's active intervention shapes a collection's potential for history making; the judgments they apply to the past reflect the present they inhabit. And the institute itself is 'a reservoir of information about the different ways film historians have perceived museum films in the past' (Lameris, 2017, p. 200). The archive is as much the result of a particular historical narrative as it as an instrument for constructing a new one. The self-reflexive stance of EYE vis-à-vis its role in shaping the historical resonance of its own collection, therefore, makes it an ideal site for the exploration of the dichotomy between canonical 'textbook' film histories and the actual material holdings in the film archive.

DICHOTOMY II: THE NEED FOR RECATEGORIZATION

Although copyright is a territorial notion, copyright law has long been the object of international regulation. The Berne Convention (1886) represents the first attempt to harmonize international copyright legislation. The UK was part of the small group of countries to first approve the treaty, while the Netherlands joined later in 1912 (the US did not join until 1989). However, despite this convention, and numerous more recent initiatives, countries continue to exhibit important differences, and copyright essentially remains national law. The purpose of this book, however, is not to provide a comparative overview of the legal circumstances of the various national film archives; rather, it focuses exclusively on the Dutch legal context.

The basic principle of Dutch copyright law (which is true of other jurisdictions as well) is that it grants the author of a work the exclusive right to reproduce and communicate its contents to the public. The rights of reproduction and communication include a range of actions, such as translation and adaptation, as well as publishing, distributing, exhibiting, and broadcasting. The period of copyright protection starts from the moment the work is created, but it does not last forever: its 'term' expires. When a copyright has expired, the work is said to be in the public domain and can be freely used without restrictions. Throughout the European Union and in the US, the length of a copyright term is currently fixed at the author's lifetime plus 70 years. After the author's death, the rights transfer to his or her heirs. However, a copyright owner may permanently 'assign' their right to another person (transferring ownership), or temporarily permit - 'licence' - another to execute copyright-restricted activities within certain limits (while retaining ownership). Licensing is the most common form of copyright exploitation. Some of the various rights known as 'moral rights' (for instance, the right to be acknowledged as the director of a film or the right to object to modification) may be retained by the author even though ownership has been assigned (Bently and Sherman, 2014).

Copyright has only come to be seen as a significant issue for institutions in the cultural sector in the last two decades, and, as a result, they began to employ specialist staff to deal with copyright problems (Padfield, 2010). For example, when EYE became the principal partner in a seven-year national digitization project, 'Images for the Future',[10] in 2007, the institute put a legal team in place, which, at its largest, consisted of four full-time employees. Ever since, EYE has been at the forefront of legal research in the film archival context and has been a partner in several international initiatives, including the European Film Gateway (EFG) project, leading a 'work package' dedicated to copyright issues, as well as the Framework for an EU-wide Audiovisual Orphan Works Registry (FORWARD).

The legal issues confronting EYE differ from those of a commercial institution. Whereas other archives can own the copyright to the large majority of their holdings, EYE, as a national public-sector institution, hardly owns any of the intellectual property of its holdings; much of its physical archive is held on deposit. The dichotomy between the intellectual ownership and material ownership of archival material, and the tension that arises with the demand for access, is most evident in a public institution, with its specific remit (and practices) of film preservation and dissemination. This issue will be looked at in more detail in later chapters.

The need to recategorize archival holdings according to their copyright-ownership status arose with the realization that the legal issues that prevent the distribution of a film 'rarely have anything to do with the type of film in question' (*A Matter of Rights*, 2010). In order to analyze the difference in how access to the materials is provided, the films need to be 'freed' from other categories, such as country, director, or genre; it is more important to know whether a film is an orphan work, for example, than whether it is a documentary (although these factors tend to be intertwined, as will emerge later). The recategorization has resulted in an archival cross section with four quadrants (reproduced below), each representing a particular copyright ownership situation plotted against its potential availability. Although the cross section has been modelled on EYE, it could also be used to represent the most common situations confronting other public-sector national archives, such as the British Film Institute (BFI) or even the Centre National du Cinéma et de l'Image Animée (CNC), the mandatory national film depository of France.

The first distinction is whether a film is still in copyright (1, 2) or whether it is in the public domain (3, 4). Within these two sections are further subdivisions. Quadrant 1 represents the films under copyright, which are more or less 'available'. Availability in the context of this cross section should be understood as the potential or latent accessibility of the material. Material might be available for researchers for an on-site consultation, for instance, but that does not mean that the material is publicly accessible for further dissemination. In the context of discovering a film's potential for 'history making', avail-

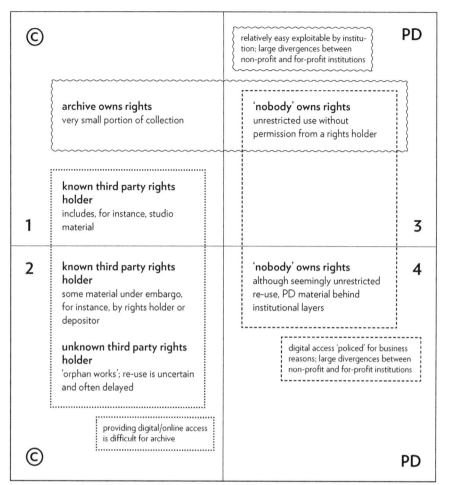

ability should be understood here as public accessibility. Quadrant 1 can be split into two parts: films to which the archive owns the rights and those with a known external third-party rights holder. The former is a very small portion of the collection and can consist of films by an individual filmmaker who has (partially) donated their holdings along with their rights to the archive. The latter includes, in the case of EYE, studio material deposited by distributors.

The second quadrant represents those films that are in copyright but are not readily available. This quadrant also consists of two sections: one with material with a known third-party rights holder, which might be under embargo (a scenario we will look at in more detail in Chapter 2), and the other with material with an unknown or un-locatable rights holder, so-called orphan works (the subject of Chapter 3). Some of the films in the orphan works section, however, after the necessary research, might turn out to be in the public domain.

Quadrants 3 and 4 can be considered together as they both address films in the public domain. As the cross section was made on the basis of copyright ownership and plotted against the material's potential availability, it could be assumed that the public domain works pose no problem as they appear legally 'available'. It turns out, however, that, although they can seemingly be reused unrestrictedly without the permission of a copyright owner, archives are not necessarily able to provide access to these materials. The exclusive ownership of the source materials plays a crucial role in this category of films, and it is where we see the largest divergences in terms of access between different types of institutions (the subject of Chapter 4).

Before turning to an analysis of the artistic practice of reusing archival film (Chapter 5), the following chapters will address each quadrant systematically, illustrating them with examples from EYE's collection. The selection of these examples has been based on the moment of their public access – between 2002 and 2005. This was a period in which the particular constellation of technological, social, economic, and institutional factors impacting the film archive and copyright remained relatively uniform. As mentioned earlier, the advantages of limiting the analysis to one institution is that most of the contextual conditions, such as institution, country, technological possibilities, and legal framework, are identical for each example and remain consistent throughout the period under scrutiny.

Although the specific way the Dutch national archive is governed, and the enormous funding opportunities for film preservation made available in the Netherlands over the last few decades, might not be representative of other regional or national film archives, the underlying legal issues in some of the examples in the following chapters represent problems that face many other archives. Films may, for example, be deposited under embargo, contradicting the archive's mandate to both preserve and to provide access to its film holdings. They might have untraceable rights owners, forcing the archive to undertake a risk analysis before deciding whether to go ahead with a particular reuse. Alternatively, films might be in the public domain and provide an opportunity for exploitation.

In terms of numbers, the second section in quadrant 1 (works in copyright with a known third-party rights holder) is by far the largest part of EYE's collection, and this arguably holds true for other national collections. Based on a database estimate, all of the other sections together – that is, the part of the collection for which the archive owns the rights, works in the public domain, plus orphan works – make up approximately less than 10% of the entire collection.[11]

Some of these works can be relatively easily exploited by the institution; some will be 'policed' for business or strategic reasons; and others can only be disseminated digitally or online after a risk assessment. There are large divergences between not-for-profit and for-profit institutions in these parts of the collection. The following chapters will look at this 10% and the consequences of the unavailability of material in greater detail, with the aim of extrapolating the more generic issues that are germane to a wider context. But, before doing so, the next chapter focuses on quadrant 1, and the first section of the second quadrant: the embargoed film.

NOTES

1   The four institutions are the Nederlands Filmmuseum, Holland Film, the Filmbank, and The Netherlands Institute for Film Education. Available at: https://www.eyefilm.nl/en/about-eye (accessed on 12 April 2016).

2   This information was provided by Leontien Bout, legal counsel for EYE, in an email to the author on 28 September 2017. The number for the BFI was provided by the BFI's legal counsel, Richard Brousson – see Estelle Derclaye (2009).

3   The funding, 13,000,000 guilders (approximately 6 million euros), was made available in two stages. It was known colloquially as 'the gold ship' (Hendriks, 1996, p. 109).

4   Although Jan de Vaal, director of the Nederlands Filmmuseum prior to Hoos Blotkamp, was a former International Federation of Film Archives (FIAF) treasurer and attended the Brighton Congress (for the list of participants, see Holman, 1982, Vol. 1, p. 365), the Filmmuseum did not contribute any film prints to the Congress (see the list in Gaudreault, 1982, Vol. 2, p. 18).

5   Available at: http://www.programma.eyefilm.nl/nieuws/in-memoriam-hoos-blotkamp (accessed on 12 April 2016).

6   The first reel, BITS & PIECES 1-11, dates from 1990. This information was provided by Annike Kross (an EYE film restorer) in an email to the author on 24 November 2014. This means, however, that the clips were assembled over a long period of time before that date.

7   To date, there have been five workshops: 'Nonfiction from the Teens' in 1994; '"Disorderly order": Colours in Silent Film' in 1995; 'The Eye of the Beholder: Exotic and Colonial Imaging' in 1998; 'Re-Assembling the Program: The Program as an Exhibition Format' in 2004; 'Advertising Films: The Images that Changed your Life' in 2009. This information was provided by Nico de Klerk, the organizer of all the workshops, in an email to the author on 22 December 2015.

8   Available at: http://en.aup.nl/series/framing-film (accessed on 28 September 2017).

9   *Fantasia of Color in Early Cinema*, a 'coffee-table book' focusing on early colour
     film images from the archives of EYE Film Institute Netherlands, was also
     published in the 'Framing Film' series in 2015.

10   Available at: http://beeldenvoordetoekomst.nl/en.html. 'Images for the future'
     was the largest digitization effort in Europe to that date.

11   This information was provided by Leontien Bout, legal counsel for EYE, in an
     email to the author on 28 September 2017.

BIBLIOGRAPHY

A Matter of Rights: A Talk with Lee Tsiantis (2010) Available at: http://selfstyledsiren.
     blogspot.ch/2010/02/matter-of-rights-talk-with-lee-tsiantis.html (accessed on 21
     April 2016).

Bently, Lionel, and Brad Sherman (2014) *Intellectual Property Law*. 4th ed. Oxford:
     Oxford University Press.

de Kuyper, Eric (1994) 'Anyone for an Aesthetics of Film History?', *Film History*, 6(1),
     pp. 100–109.

Delpeut, Peter (1998) *Juryrapport Sphinx Cultuurprijs 1998*. Maastricht: N.V. Konink-
     lijke Sphinx Gustavsberg, pp. 1–5.

Delpeut, Peter (2012) 'An Unexpected Reception. LYRICAL NITRATE Between Film
     History and Art', in Marente Bloemheuvel, Giovanna Fossati, and Jaap Gulde-
     mond (eds.) *Found Footage. Cinema Exposed*. Amsterdam: Amsterdam University
     Press/EYE Film Institute Netherlands, pp. 218–224.

Derclaye, Estelle (ed.) (2009) *BILETA conference*. The University of Winchester Law
     School, 30 March [Online]. Available at: http://works.bepress.com/cgi/
     viewcontent.cgi?article=1023&context=estelle_derclaye (accessed on 21 April
     2016).

Fernandez Escareño, Itzia (2009) *La Compilation. Un Outil Paradoxal de Valorisation des
     Films Muets Recyclés par Peter Delpeut et Coproduits par le Nederlands Filmmuseum
     (1989-1999)*. PhD Dissertation. Université Sorbonne Nouvelle – Paris 3.

Fossati, Giovanna (2009) *From Grain to Pixel: The Archival Life of Film in Transition*.
     Amsterdam: Amsterdam University Press.

Fossati, Giovanna (2012) 'Found Footage. Filmmaking, Film Archiving and New
     Participatory Platforms', in Marente Bloemheuvel, Giovanna Fossati, and Jaap
     Guldemond (eds.) *Found Footage. Cinema Exposed*. Amsterdam: Amsterdam
     University Press/EYE Film Institute Netherlands, pp. 177–184.

Gaudreault, André (ed.) (1982) *Cinema 1900-1906. Part 2: Filmography*. Brussels: Inter-
     national Federation of Film Archives (FIAF).

Hendriks, Annemieke (1996) *Huis van illusies. De geschiedenis van paviljoen Vondelpark
     en het Nederlands Filmmuseum*. Amsterdam: Bas Lubberhuizen.

48 |

Hertogs, Daan, and Nico de Klerk (eds.) (1994) *Nonfiction from the Teens. The 1994 Amsterdam Workshop*. Amsterdam: Stichting Nederlands Filmmuseum.

Hertogs, Daan, and Nico de Klerk (eds.) (1996) *Disorderly Order: Colours in Silent Film. The 1995 Amsterdam Workshop*. Amsterdam: Stichting Nederlands Filmmuseum.

Holman, Roger (ed.) (1982) *Cinema 1900-1906. Part 1: An Analytical Study by the National Film Archive (London) and the International Federation of Film Archives*. Brussels: International Federation of Film Archives (FIAF).

Meyer, Mark-Paul (2012) 'From the Archive and Other Contexts', in Marente Bloemheuvel, Giovanna Fossati, and Jaap Guldemond (eds.) *Found Footage. Cinema Exposed*. Amsterdam: Amsterdam University Press/EYE Film Institute Netherlands, pp. 145-152.

Padfield, Tim (2010) 'Preserving and Accessing our Cultural Heritage – Issues for Cultural Sector Institutions: Archives, Libraries, Museums and Galleries', in Estelle Derclaye (ed.) *Copyright and Cultural Heritage. Preservation and Access to Works in a Digital World*. Cheltenham: Edward Elgar Publishing, pp. 195-209.

ABOUT THE AUTHOR

Claudy Op den Kamp is Lecturer in Film and faculty member at the Centre for Intellectual Property Policy and Management at Bournemouth University, UK, and Adjunct Research Fellow at Swinburne Law School, Australia.

CHAPTER 2

A Swiss Bank

Recategorization I – The embargoed film

Op den Kamp, Claudy, *The Greatest Films Never Seen. The Film Archive and the Copyright Smokescreen*. Amsterdam University Press, 2018

| 51

DOI: 10.5117/9789462981393_CH02

ABSTRACT

This chapter, using the recategorization suggested in Chapter 1, commences with a systematic analysis of digital access to films that fall within a public sector archive's legal cross section, introduced in Chapter 1. Examples show that, while copyright fulfils a protective function for rights holders, it can limit a film's potential for 'history making' by inhibiting its public accessibility.

KEYWORDS
embargoed collections, rights holders, ALS TWEE DRUPPELS WATER, colourization debate

ALS TWEE DRUPPELS WATER (NL 1963, Dir. Fons Rademakers)
(courtesy of EYE Film Institute)

This chapter, using the recategorization suggested in the previous chapter, commences a systematic analysis of digital access to those films that fall into the quadrants of a public-sector archive's legal cross section (see the chart in Chapter 1). It marks the beginning of an exploration throughout the next few chapters of the impact of copyright on the visibility of important works that are arguably crucial to our understanding of the past and the history of film.

In one of these instances, the film archive itself could be described as a sort of 'Swiss bank'. The film archivist and cofounder of the Cinémathèque française, Henri Langlois (cited in Houston, 1994, p. 49), described the archive in similar terms when he spoke of its 'obligation to maintain confidentiality about its holdings in the interests of its depositors'. The chapter looks at Fons Rademakers' 1963 film, ALS TWEE DRUPPELS WATER ('LIKE TWO DROPS OF WATER'), an embargoed work in the Nederlands Filmmuseum's collection, which exemplifies the copyright dichotomy between material and intellectual property that such a characterization presupposes. It also draws a comparison with an international example of this dichotomy: the colourization debate of the late 1980s in the US.

Both examples expose the archive as a vulnerable place, unable to guarantee a fixed and stable environment for cinematic memories. They also show that while copyright fulfils a protective function for rights holders, it can limit a film's potential for 'history making' by inhibiting its public accessibility.

THE ARCHIVE AS RIGHTS HOLDER

The first and most obvious result of a legal cross section of an audiovisual archive is that it falls into two parts: films in copyright (quadrants 1 and 2) and films out of copyright (quadrants 3 and 4). In the European Union and the US, copyright currently lasts for a term of 70 years beyond the author's death, and, although there are many exceptions, this very generally means that most films are still in copyright. In most public-sector but also in privately held archives, such works will comprise the majority of the holdings. This chapter and the next study the films in copyright, while Chapter 4 examines those out of copyright.

A further division can be made based on whether the copyright is held by the archive or by a third party. A commercial archive, such as a studio archive, will own the rights to the large majority of its holdings. When a secure copyright ownership is in place that will protect against potential infringement when the film is distributed, it is relatively straightforward to initiate a film restoration project that requires a substantial initial investment as the investor can expect to benefit financially when the film is made public. The restoration of David Lean's THE BRIDGE ON THE RIVER KWAI (1957) in 2010 and Martin Scorsese's TAXI DRIVER (1976) in 2011 by their copyright owner, Sony Pictures Entertainment, are recent examples.

The public-sector archive (the physical context for this analysis) presents a very different scenario: it holds the rights to very few of its holdings.[1] When large parties donate or deposit films, the rights are not usually transferred (Rother, 2014). Distributors tend to deposit multiple copies of (feature) films in the archive systematically after their theatrical run is over, but only on rare occasions are the rights to this material transferred with the donation or deposit.

Nowadays, the contract between donor and archive generally lays down specific limitations. In the case of EYE, the archive has reached contractual agreements with certain filmmakers and collections, whereby, for instance, potential profits will be shared; however, only very few production companies have transferred all of the exclusive rights to their films to the archive.[2]

In the context of a public-sector archive, the part of the collection that is owned by the archive is almost negligible; the vast majority of the collection will be owned by someone else.

THIRD-PARTY RIGHTS HOLDERS: FRAGILE RELATIONS

In his account of European film archiving in the 1950s, the cofounder of the Cinémathèque de Toulouse, Raymond Borde (1983, p. 121, author's translation), describes the 'arrival of a redoubtable character in the sleepy and peaceful landscape where the film archives reside: the rights holder'. For several decades, rights holders were regarded with suspicion; Borde refers to them as 'alligators' hiding in the swamps where archives 'peacefully conduct their historic mission of cultural preservation' (1983, p. 121). The time that Borde depicts is one in which the default attitude of film archives was secrecy (de Kuyper, 2013). The relationship between archives and commercial producers could be characterized as contentious. The producers, who were often the copyright holders, could legally confiscate materials that had been acquired by less-than-legal means. Many archives therefore resorted to concealment, and most of these institutions did not have a full or accessible catalogue.

However, the 1980s saw a new generation of archivists take the helm at the major archives, who brought to their work a higher degree of transparency and a sense of collaboration that also extended to their relationships with third-party rights holders (de Kuyper, 2013).

The second part of quadrant 1 – those film holdings with a known third-party copyright holder – arguably comprises a very large part of most archives' collections. In general, a public-sector archive can collect, preserve, and provide on-site access to films that have third-party rights holders, but cannot distribute them commercially or engage in other projects without the specific permission of the rights holder. When a film has a known copyright holder, however, it is clear whom to ask for permission to reuse the film material. That is not to say that permission will necessarily be forthcoming, but at least negotiations can be set in motion.

EYE, for instance, collaborates in international projects to restore film elements that are in their keeping but to which they do not hold the rights. In such cases, an external party, such as another archive or producer, will initiate the restoration project and ideally clear the copyright with the rights holders. In exchange for lending some of their film elements, EYE receives an attribution in the credits or a restoration copy for its own collection. A recent example of this is Alfred Hitchcock's DOWNHILL (1927), restored in collaboration with the BFI in 2012. Another common scenario involves EYE supporting another archive's restoration project, where the material it holds is out of copyright – for example, Alfred Machin's MAUDITE SOIT LA GUERRE (WAR IS HELL, 1914), restored in collaboration with Belgium's Cinémathèque royale in 2014.

It is fairly normal for a contract to be drawn up between the donating party and the archive specifying the conditions attached to a particular donation or deposit, including limitations on the access to and distribution of the film. The role of the archive, however, is called into question when the rights holder stipulates that access to the material is indefinitely suspended, keeping the film out of the public realm. When films are publicly inaccessible, their ability to engage with the dynamics of history and to fulfil their potential for 'history making' are greatly limited.

Close-up: ALS TWEE DRUPPELS WATER ('LIKE TWO DROPS OF WATER')

Fons Rademakers' celebrated film, ALS TWEE DRUPPELS WATER (1963), remained under embargo in the Nederlands Filmmuseum, due to the copyright holder's restrictions, for nearly four decades, despite the archive's remit of preservation, restoration, and dissemination.

The story behind this state of affairs begins with Rademakers' search for additional financing to supplement the funding given to him by the national Productiefonds voor Nederlandse Film (Production Fund for Dutch Films) to make the film. He approached several rich industrialists and ultimately found a partner in beer tycoon Freddy Heineken, who was looking to break into film production and therefore offered to fund the whole film himself (Barten, 2002). By financing and producing ALS TWEE DRUPPELS WATER, Heineken became the film's rights holder.

The film was an international success, not least due to the work of cameraman Raoul Coutard, who had recently contributed to such hits as Jean-Luc Godard's À BOUT DE SOUFFLE (1960) and François Truffaut's JULES ET JIM (1962) (Welgraven, 2001). The film played at the 1963 International Film Festival in Cannes, alongside such films as Visconti's IL GATTOPARDO and Fellini's OTTO E MEZZO, where it was nominated for a Golden Palm (Barten, 2002). Soon afterwards, however, Heineken withdrew it from circulation, allegedly in retaliation against an ex-girlfriend who had played a minor role in the film. In search of more control over his creative efforts, Rademakers tried to buy the film's rights from Heineken, but his request was rejected. As a result, what was considered, according to Dutch newspaper *Het Parool*, a 'courageous film noir of European stature' (Barten, 2002) vanished into the vaults of the Nederlands Filmmuseum. The reason why Heineken withdrew the film is relatively unimportant, and the story itself is clouded in obscurity; however, the fact that he was able to do so – much to the chagrin of the director – is significant.

The film was rarely seen after its withdrawal from public viewing. It was screened a few times on special occasions – at a retrospective of Rademakers' work, for example – but only with Heineken's express permission. The film was also screened occasionally at Heineken's private viewings. However, there were no further public cinema or television screenings. In the 1980s, Heineken obstructed the film's television broadcast, ostensibly so that he would not miss out on potential home-video revenues (van Driel, 2003). Rademakers, in turn, learnt from his experience with ALS TWEE DRUPPELS WATER and produced all his subsequent films himself (Beerekamp, 2002). In the future, as the rights holder, he would be in charge of the fate of his films.

In the meantime, the Nederlands Filmmuseum shouldered the financial responsibility for the continued preservation of the film's source material without any possibility of providing access to the film itself. When Heineken died in early 2002, archivists at the museum reopened negotiations with his heirs, who agreed to the restoration and redistribution of the film (van Bracht, 2012). The restored film re-premièred in September 2003, at the Nederlands Film Festival in Utrecht, after nearly 40 years' absence from the public realm and erasure from the (Dutch) audience's collective memory, and only a few years before Rademakers died.

The film itself has been heralded for its complex portrayal of the Second World War, particularly when compared with other films of the era. Like the 1958 book it adapted (*The Darkroom of Damocles* by Willem Frederik Hermans), it questions reality, the nature of betrayal and resistance, and whether morally correct choices are possible in extreme circumstances (Schoots, 2004). ALS TWEE DRUPPELS WATER is now considered one of the most important postwar Dutch feature films.

The colourization debate

Although some of the circumstances of the 'colourization debate' differ significantly from the previous example of an embargoed film (the debate mainly played out in a commercial setting and the rights of the films were sold to the owner of that commercial setting), it reflects the same struggle between the rights holders, who call the shots, and the directors, who lack any power over their work. However, in this case, the heirs of one of the directors involved were able, by means of a European court ruling based on his moral rights, to halt the use of colour – although he did not live to see the results.

Although experiments with colourization had been taking place for some years, the controversy really picked up speed when media mogul Ted Turner bought the MGM and RKO film libraries in 1986 and 1987, respectively. The purchase included the copyright to the films, and Turner quickly announced that he wanted to colourize them. Films originally shot (and instilled in the audience's collective memory) in black and white were colourized with the help of digital technology. A video copy of the film was colourized, while the original black-and-white film elements were left 'untouched':

> The team's first task was to take the best available copy of the film and transfer it to one-inch videotape. For the purpose, Turner had a freshly minted print struck from the original negative. This pristine celluloid copy was then dubbed onto videotape, and a digital computer was used to further enhance the picture by removing any discernible blemishes. (Edgerton, 2000, p. 28)

Colour titles were in high demand for television screenings: it was believed they would stop people from channel-hopping (allegedly more prevalent with black-and-white films), and could be programmed in prime time (Slide, 1992). Moreover, Turner could distribute the materials on his own television channels. The Turner Entertainment Company represented a gigantic 'corporate coalition that controlled both the copyrights and the ancillary markets' (Edgerton, 2000, p. 25), so potential returns were high.

However, it seems that the decision to colourize these films was fuelled by an arguably more significant factor. A large amount of the black-and-white titles were about to enter the public domain, but, as colourized, derivative works, they would be granted another 75 years of copyright protection:

> One of the major advantages of the colorization process and its competitors was that by adding color to black-and-white films, it was possible to copyright them as *new* titles, thus adding additional years of copyright life to a copyright protected black-and-white feature and starting a whole new copyright life for a film already in the public domain. Of course, the colorization process [did] not affect the copyright status of the black-and-white original. (Slide, 1992, p. 124)

In July 1988, the Library of Congress confirmed the difference between the colour-converted CASABLANCA and the 1942 Michael Curtiz original by awarding a new copyright to the Turner Entertainment Company. This decision determined that the addition of a minimum of three colours to a black-and-white film was all that was needed to legally copyright the new version as a separate work (Edgerton, 2000).

Colourization, as a method of extending the duration of copyright protection, reveals the copyright holder as the most powerful party in terms of the title's public accessibility, irrespective of who owns the film 'creatively' or materially. Colour conversion and a new copyright made the practice seem a profitable enterprise:

> It's only feasible to convert to color if you own the world rights, since the cost would be prohibitive for small markets. [...] [Turner] might have hesitated to pay 1.2 billion USD for a film library if the pictures had soon lapsed into the public domain. By converting them to color, though, he could get a fresh copyright, which would be valuable for years to come in the broadcast and cassette markets. [...] [T]he companies were trying to conjure private property out of the public domain. (Klawans, 1990, p. 175)

The justifications *for* colourization often took a teleological turn. It was argued that, if the original filmmakers had been able to, they would have shot the films in colour. This argument was based on the underlying (untrue) idea that a black-and-white title was essentially a primitive version of a colour film. Initially, many filmmakers were interested in the process; Frank Capra, for instance, was an early adopter. When it became clear, however, that the directors' permission was not needed before embarking on the colourizing process, since, in most cases, they were not the rights holders or the film had already lapsed into the public domain, most of them turned vehemently against the practice.[3]

The arguments *against* colourization included ethical aspects. The practice was seen to condone a so-called 'falsification' of history:

> Films made in the black and white era capture and record the heritage and culture of a time now passed. To present altered versions of these films, it is said, is akin to presenting an altered version of American history. Instead of educating the young as to the worth of these original films and their era, colorized films instead present a faddish and distorted view of history. (Kohs, 1988, p. 36)

Anthony Slide (1992, p. 127) explains that copyright holders were thought to have an 'ethical responsibility' to protect and preserve the artistic integrity of black-and-white films. Colourization was seen as 'cultural vandalism and a distortion of history' and an 'unwarranted intrusion into the artistry of the cinematographer' (Slide, 1992, p. 129). In their arguments against the practice, filmmakers focused on the rights of the mass audience, whose sensibilities would be 'corrupted' if they were deprived of the original black-and-white versions (Edgerton, 2000, p. 27).

Turner relished the controversy and welcomed all sorts of accusations, provocatively telling reporters at a press conference in the summer of 1988 that he 'colorized CASABLANCA just to piss everybody off. [...] I wanted to do it and it's mine' (Slide, 1992, p. 126). The audience, however, did not seem to care that much: they watched the broadcasts and they bought the videotapes, but, by the early 1990s, the novelty had worn off and they lost interest; colourized videos rapidly became money losers (Edgerton, 2000).

A more significant issue in the colourization controversy, however, is embedded in the question of the artist's moral rights. David Kohs (1988, p. 28) shows how '[t]he fundamental difference between the American and European systems of copyright was brought to the forefront by the colorization controversy': one system favours ownership, the other the creative person behind the work. The crux of the controversy has often been expressed as essentially 'one of ownership versus creative rights' (p. 7).[4] The legal situation in Europe, with its focus on moral rights, stipulates that the maker (who is not necessarily the rights holder) may limit the ways in which and by whom the work is presented, and can object to any distortion or modification that might constitute a misrepresentation of their artistic vision.

John Huston's heirs, for instance, fought to obstruct the broadcast of a colourized version of his MGM-produced film, THE ASPHALT JUNGLE (1950). Turner had the film colourized, and, because the US does not recognize the moral rights of the director, Huston's heirs could not prevent its domestic broadcast. Indeed, as the director, Huston had no legal claim over the film in the US at all; initially, the rights were MGM's. When the film was scheduled to be broadcast in France, a country that does legally recognize moral rights, Huston's heirs took the case to the French courts. The final ruling came too late to prevent the film's broadcast in 1988, but, in 1994, 'a French trial court permanently banned the television broadcast of a colourized version of John Huston's THE ASPHALT JUNGLE on the basis that it would cause "unmendable and intolerable damage" to the integrity of the work and would therefore compromise Huston's moral rights' (Grainge, 1999, p. 636). Moreover, the court ruled that all directors are considered coauthors, and so these rights could be passed on to the heirs (Vaidyanathan, 2017) – a ruling that was particularly important in this case as Huston had died by this time.

A 'DISTORTION' OF FILM HISTORY

Film archives have preserved and restored colour films in black and white for several decades now as part of an established preservation and restoration practice, driven by budgetary and long-term chemical stability concerns (Read and Meyer, 2000). Although film scholars have addressed these preservation processes as historical practices,[5] they have (surprisingly) never considered them in a film-historical context as a possible distortion of film history.

Similarly, as motion pictures have been a television staple for decades, distortions and alterations, such as panning and scanning,[6] lexiconning,[7] and other editing functions, have been routinely used to present theatrical films in a televisual format (Kohs, 1988). Again, however, although these practices are creatively controversial in their own right and are often opposed by the filmmakers themselves, they have not been framed in a scholarly context as potentially misrepresenting film history.

So why did the inverse of the standard archival practice, the colourization of black-and-white films, create such a controversy? Was it the obvious interference of the rights holders? Was it perhaps the realization that the archive could no longer be seen as a safe haven for an 'official' film history? Colourization created new versions that could be protected by copyright and there was a real concern that it was these colour versions that would live on rather than the black-and-white versions so familiar to audiences. The idea that certain titles could only be accessed in a form or version that differs dramatically from the way the film is generally remembered shook the very idea of what a film archive is. Rather than a place of preservation that lends a certain stability to a film's memory, it came to be seen as a mere warehouse for copyright holders' property, a 'Swiss bank'.

THE NATIONAL FILM REGISTRY

One of the outcomes of the colourization controversy in the US was the establishment of a national film commission tasked with creating a National Film Registry – that is, a canon of distinguished films: 'The National Film Preservation Act, part of a Department of the Interior appropriations bill, create[d] a 13-member panel that could name up to 25 movies a year to be included in a national registry of classic films' (*New York Times*, 1988). These would be 'culturally, historically, or aesthetically significant films' (Slide, 1992, p. 131) that would showcase the range and diversity of American film heritage and increase awareness of the need for its preservation. Although the Act's primary purpose was to stop colourization and other reformatting processes, the conflation of ideas of preservation and ownership are interesting to note, and it is questionable whether its name actually reflects its supposed remit:

> The name of the bill [The National Film Preservation Act] is, of course, a misnomer. It has nothing whatsoever to do with film preservation. All the bill does is have the Librarian of Congress, in collaboration with his appointed panel, select 25 films a year which can still be altered in any way by their copyright owners. (Slide, 1992, p. 131)

The Act could not (and cannot) protect the 'safety' of the film titles; it was only able to force copyright holders to indicate on the film itself if it had been reformatted or otherwise changed since its original release. As Kohs (1988, p. 19) remarks, the 'longest anyone would be able to thwart the colorization process would be a period equal to the duration of the copyright in the film itself. After this period [...] the film falls into the public domain and anyone [with access to a material copy] is free to make a colorized version'.

THE 'REAL' QUESTION

The real question underpinning the colourization controversy seems to be: what exactly is 'official' film history and where does it reside? Some of the fears mentioned above might even be justified. Given the enormous financial investment required for colourization, 'it is likely to be the colored version, which will, perhaps exclusively, be marketed. The public cannot [easily] go into the archive and see the original black and white print. As a result, original black and white works might indeed be effectively replaced by colorized copies' (Kohs, 1988, p. 30). Not all of the filmic evidence that is kept in the archives can be publicly viewed or used; the colourization debate made it obvious that, just because a film is extant does not necessarily mean it is publicly accessible. Helene Roberts (1994) argues that images that were first seen are the ones that persist in the memory, so colourization's threat was that now some of the material would be made publicly accessible, but in a completely different form than the original.

The colourization debate brought into focus the powerful position of the rights holder, as well as the dichotomy between intellectual and material ownership – especially when the holders of these rights are one and the same – and the repercussions for what could be called the audience's 'cultural' ownership. Although amending intellectual property holdings has always been the prerogative of studios and producers, the archive was now exposed as a vulnerable place for archived films:

> [T]he innovative technologies that brought about the ability to replicate and exhibit films inexpensively also created the capacity for people outside of the archival setting to alter the content and meanings of canonical films. [...] Colorization technology also revealed a significant and troubling fact about the cinematic artefact: powerful people and new technologies could dramatically alter films sitting safely in the archive. The film archive [...] hardly guarantees a fixed and stable cinematic memoryscape. (Jones, 2012, pp. 18-19)

Thus, the archive found itself on shaky ground, and, as a result, so too did the writing of film history, since 'filmic meaning was not necessarily tied to or correlated with the cinematic artefact protected in the archival vault' (p. 78). What colourization emphasized is that the film archive 'could not maintain, protect, or help to construct a singular cinematic meaning for any film' (p. 78). It threatened the established position of the film archive and undermined its status (and that of its films) as a primary historical source.

This chapter has explored two examples of how the dichotomy between material and intellectual property plays out: one in which both rights are held by the same party and one in which they are not. These examples also take place in two vastly divergent contexts. The situation of an embargoed film in a public-sector archive, with its mandate to preserve and provide access to its holdings, is very different from the circumstances of a film in the hands of a powerful rights holder, who inventively prolongs copyright on his intellectual property, and, in the process (perhaps unwittingly), rewrites film history.

The next chapter turns to the subject of 'orphan films' – that is, films that are still within the copyright period but lack an identifiable or locatable rights holder, and which raise particular difficulties in the context of the debate on archival access.

NOTES

1   There are other exceptions for which no permission is needed, but these lie outside the scope of this book.

2   This information was provided by Ronny Temme (former head of sales at Nederlands Filmmuseum/EYE) by email on 1 February 2014, and by Leontien Bout (EYE's legal counsel) in a phone conversation on 13 March 2014.

3   Directors spearheading the crusade against colourization included Frank Capra, Woody Allen, and John Huston, amongst others. Orson Welles, on the other hand, was able to rely on a clause in his contract that prevented anyone tampering with his work to forestall the colourization of CITIZEN KANE (Slide, 1992).

4   A current version of the same debate can be seen in what has been dubbed 'dimensionalization', converting films to 3D (Hoyt, 2011).

5   See, for instance, Bregt Lameris (2007; 2017).

6   This is a process by which theatrical motion pictures, composed for viewing on large screens, are altered to fit the narrower television screen (USCO, 1989).

7   This technology involves the electronic time compression or expansion of a motion picture in order to fit the picture into a broadcasting time slot (USCO, 1989).

BIBLIOGRAPHY

Barten, Egbert (2002) 'Een verloren klassieker', *Skrien*, 34(8), pp. 22–24.

Beerekamp, Hans (2002) 'Wie kent de film van Freddy?', *NRC Handelsblad*, 4 January 2002.

Borde, Raymond (1983) *Les Cinémathèques*. Lausanne: Editions L'Age d'Homme.

Bracht, Maarten van (2012) 'Freddy's motieven' [Online]. Available at: http://boeken.vpro.nl/artikelen/2012/oktober/de-donkere-kamer-van-damokles.html (accessed on 27 April 2014).

de Kuyper, Eric (2013) 'Werken bij een Filmarchief/Filmmuseum, of: Schizofrenie als opdracht', in: Cinemathèque royale de Belgique (ed.) *75000 Films*. Crisnée: Editions Yellow Now, pp. 121–137.

Edgerton, Gary (2000) 'The Germans Wore Gray, You Wore Blue: Frank Capra, Casablanca, and the Colorization Controversy of the 1980s', *Journal of Popular Film and Television,* 27(4), pp. 24–32.

Grainge, Paul (1999) 'Reclaiming Heritage: Colourization, Culture Wars and the Politics of Nostalgia', *Cultural Studies*, 13(4), pp. 621–638.

Houston, Penelope (1994) *Keepers of the Frame: The Film Archives*. London: British Film Institute.

Hoyt, Eric (2011) 'The Future of Selling the Past; Studio Libraries in the 21st Century', *ejumpcut*, [Online]. Available at: http://www.ejumpcut.org/archive/jc52.2010/hoytStudioLibraries/ (accessed on 21 April 2016).

Klawans, Stuart (1990) 'Rose-Tinted Spectacles', in Mark Crispin Miller (ed.) *Seeing Through Movies*. New York: Pantheon Books, pp. 150–185.

Kohs, David (1988) 'Paint Your Wagon-Please!: Colorization, Copyright, and the Search for Moral Rights', *Federal Communications Law Journal*, 40, pp. 1–38.

Lameris, Bregt (2007) *Opnieuw belicht: de pas de deux tussen de filmmuseale praktijk en filmhistorische debatten*. PhD Dissertation, Universiteit Utrecht.

Lameris, Bregt (2017) *Film Museum Practice and Film Historiography. The Case of the Nederlands Filmmuseum (1946-2000)*. Amsterdam: Amsterdam University Press.

NYT (1988), 'Reagan Signs Law on Film', *New York Times*, 28 September 1988.

Read, Paul, and Mark-Paul Meyer (eds.) (2000) *Restoration of Motion Picture Film*. Oxford: Butterworth-Heinemann.

Roberts, Helene (1994) 'Second Hand Images: The Role of Surrogates in Artistic and Cultural Exchange', *Visual Resources*, 9(4), pp. 335-346.

Rother, Rainer (2014) *Filmhistorisches Arbeiten am Museum* [Lecture Forschungskolloquium FIWI, University of Zurich]. 15 October.

Schoots, Hans (2004) *Van Fanfare tot Spetters. Een cultuurgeschiedenis van de jaren zestig en zeventig*. Amsterdam: Uitgeverij Bas Lubberhuizen.

Slide, Anthony (1992) *Nitrate Won't Wait: A History of Film Preservation in the United States*. Jefferson: McFarland & Company.

United States Copyright Office (USCO) (1989) Technological Alterations to Motion Pictures and Other Audiovisual Works: Implications for Creators, Copyright Owners and Consumers. Report of the Register of Copyrights. [Online]. Available at: http://digitalcommons.lmu.edu/elr/vol10/iss1/1/ (accessed on 10 March 2015).

Vaidhyanathan, Siva (2017) *Intellectual Property. A Very Short Introduction*. Oxford: Oxford University Press.

van Driel, Anne (2003) 'Ach, zo'n gerucht doet het goed voor de film', *de Volkskrant,* 23 August 2003.

Welgraven, Co (2001) '...ging ALS TWEE DRUPPELS WATER achter slot en grendel', *Trouw*, 26 March 2001.

| 63

ABOUT THE AUTHOR

Claudy Op den Kamp is Lecturer in Film and faculty member at the Centre for Intellectual Property Policy and Management at Bournemouth University, UK, and Adjunct Research Fellow at Swinburne Law School, Australia.

CHAPTER 3

A Handbag

Recategorization II – The orphan film

Op den Kamp, Claudy, *The Greatest Films Never Seen. The Film Archive* | 65
and the Copyright Smokescreen. Amsterdam University Press, 2018

DOI: 10.5117/9789462981393_CH03

ABSTRACT

This chapter addresses the issue of so-called orphan works – films with no known rights holders, and considers the definition, scope, and some of the underlying causes of the orphan works problem, as well as a number of proposed solutions. An example from EYE's collection will demonstrate how the search for rights holders can significantly delay the distribution of an archival film.

KEYWORDS
DE OVERVAL, unknown rights holders, orphan works problem, orphan works directive

DE OVERVAL (NL 1962, Dir. Paul Rotha)
(courtesy of EYE Film Institute)

The indifference of the film industry to its past products, and the neglect, loss, decay, or willful destruction of these works, as well as other political, economic, and curatorial factors, have helped define which of the fragmentary group of archival films are available to study. As Chapter 2 has shown, copyright ownership can be added to the list of historical and contemporary factors that influence what material is publicly accessible.

This chapter continues the debate by addressing the second part of quadrant 2: the issue of so-called orphan works – films with no known rights holders. In fact, some of these elusive rights holders might not even be aware of their ownership rights themselves. In addition to its negative impact on the archival material's (film) historical role, copyright (in the case of orphan works) also restricts the potential remuneration of rights holders – a double bind. The chapter considers the definition, scope, and some of the underlying causes of the orphan works problem, as well as a number of proposed solutions.

An example from EYE's collection will demonstrate how the search for rights holders can significantly delay the distribution of an archival film, and the chapter goes on to explore how the problem of orphan films reveals the workings of the archival institution. The film archive is the context in which these problems arise, yet the archive itself – including the human agency of its archivists – has figured little in the academic debate on archival access. This chapter aims to address this gap in the research.

CLOSE-UP: *DE OVERVAL* ('*THE SILENT RAID*')

Paul Rotha's 1962 film, DE OVERVAL, tells the story of a raid on a Gestapo-run detention centre in the northern Dutch town of Leeuwarden in 1944: a small group of resistance fighters entered the prison and liberated 51 of their comrades. DE OVERVAL holds a special place in Dutch (film) history as the first feature film to portray the Dutch resistance movement.

In 2003, the Nederlands Filmmuseum, in collaboration with the Frisian Resistance Museum, decided to distribute DE OVERVAL on DVD. The Frisian museum had a predominantly local constituency of interested consumers with an appetite for the film, while the Nederlands Filmmuseum held the physical prints. The project had in fact been attempted several times before, but each time it was stalled by the failure to answer the vexed question of the film's copyright ownership. As publishing the film on DVD would entail reproducing the work and communicating it to the public, both copyright-restricted activities, the rights holder's permission was a legal requisite. However, although DE OVERVAL was a well-known Dutch film, it was not immediately clear who owned the rights or how to retrieve this information.

There had been previous attempts to trace the copyright owner, without result. This does not mean that the film had not been reused, but each reuse involved a time-consuming 'risk assessment' to establish whether it was worth reusing the film in a particular context without first clearing the rights. However, as the previous incidental reuses – an exhibition at the Frisian Resistance Museum and educational screenings in schools – were mostly of a noncommercial nature, the Nederlands Filmmuseum handled the request to help distribute the film commercially on DVD with more caution.

First, it was necessary to establish whether the film was actually still in copyright. Article 40 of the Dutch copyright law (the Auteurswet) states:

> The copyright in a film work expires 70 years after the first of January of the year following the year in which the last of the following persons to survive died: the principal director, the author of the screenplay, the author of the dialogue and he who created the music for the film work. (Eechoud, in Hugenholtz et al., 2012, p. 535)[1]

The film's producer, Rudolf Meyer, had founded his production company, Sapphire Film Producties N.V., in 1958. Aside from DE OVERVAL, it produced two other Dutch feature films: Bert Haanstra's FANFARE in 1958 and Kees Brusse's MENSEN VAN MORGEN ('PEOPLE OF TOMORROW') in 1964. Sapphire approached Rotha (a writer, producer, and director, as well as a pioneer of the British documentary movement and head of documentaries at the BBC between 1953 and 1955) to direct the fact-based feature film. But, as the company was concerned that the film might not retain its Dutch character with an English director at the helm, it also asked Kees Brusse, a well-known Dutch actor and director, not only to star in the film but also to direct the Dutch dialogue.

However, of the four possible authors of the film whose presence would legally determine the length of copyright protection, the only one still alive in 2003 was the writer of the screenplay, Louis de Jong. He had outlived the principal director (although Brusse's input was extensive, Rotha was the overall director), the author of the dialogue (Rotha and de Jong both have writing credits), and the composer of the film's music (Else van Epen-de Groot). As de Jong was still alive, the film was therefore still within the copyright period.[2]

This was where the real detective work began. The first step in the process was to determine the identity of the film's first copyright owner, and from there to pursue the trail to the current rights holder. The author is normally the first copyright owner, but Article 7 of the Auteurswet states:

> Where labour which is carried out in the service of another consists in the making of certain literary, scientific or artistic works, the person in whose service the works were created is taken to be the maker, unless the parties have agreed otherwise. (Eechoud, in Hugenholtz et al., 2012, p. 508)

Although specific contracts were missing, Sapphire, as the production company, was probably the film's first copyright owner. However, trade papers at the Chamber of Commerce in Amsterdam revealed that the production company had gone bankrupt in 1973 and was subsequently purchased by Tuschinski Film Distributie.[3] Assuming that Sapphire *was* the first rights owner, the next step was to determine what had happened to the company's assets after its purchase. The trade papers contained potentially instrumental information, such as the names of the former owners and the bankruptcy administrators, but none of the contact details were up-to-date.

The trail also led to less official sources, including numerous individuals connected in some way to the film and its production company – for example, the former owners of Tuschinski and their children (possible heirs to the copyright); the archivist at Pathé, the company that currently owns the Tuschinski archive; and the directors of other films produced by Sapphire, as well as their children. It would not have been an unusual legal move if, during Sapphire's bankruptcy process, the filmmakers were offered the opportunity to buy back the copyright to their own films. Tracing what had happened to the two other feature films that the company produced could unearth essential information regarding this eventuality.

Brusse not only directed the Dutch dialogues in DE OVERVAL, but was also the principal director of MENSEN VAN MORGEN, the third feature produced by Sapphire – and he was the only one of the three directors who was still alive. Already advanced in years and living in Australia, Brusse nevertheless attended a retrospective that the Nederlands Filmmuseum organized in 2005 to celebrate his 80th birthday. When the author met him at the event and asked him about these films, Brusse initially agreed that he probably was the rights holder to both films, but he could not give a definitive answer. He was not the only one in the dark. As the director of Bert Haanstra Films B.V., Haanstra's son Rimko distributes his father's film, FANFARE, but he also did not know who owns the film's copyright,[4] although he continues to charge a handling fee for distributing the film until a copyright owner comes forward. Given this information, it appeared that the filmmakers were not offered the opportunity to buy the rights to their own films. Tracing Rotha's heirs – which might well have been complicated, not least because he was an only child and was himself childless – was therefore deemed an interesting but possibly diversionary endeavor best left to future researchers.

Meyer, the film's producer, died in 1969, and no up-to-date contact information for his only daughter (who was believed to live in Germany) was available. Indeed, Céline Linssen, former editor-in-chief of Dutch film magazines *Skrien* and *Versus*, had planned to write a book about Meyer but abandoned the idea after she found he had not left behind enough official traces on which to base a monograph.

The investigation therefore expanded to encompass the companies that distributed copies of the film and the archives that possessed film prints and donation files. It seemed likely that information held in these records and a possible financial trail could help untangle the complex chain of rights holders. The British Film Institute (BFI) holds the film copies of THE SILENT RAID, the English remake of DE OVERVAL. The film's donation file stated that Tuschinski donated the film to the BFI in 1973. The question was: did the company donate the film because it wanted to redistribute its newly acquired property and thought that the BFI would be the best home for the prints of the English version? However, the answer to this was complicated by the fact that Tuschinski did not need to own the rights to the film in order to donate it. Although, as the owner of the physical work, the company would not have the immediate right to copy the film, it would have the right to sell (or even destroy) it.

Gofilex, a Dutch distribution company that distributed a 16mm copy of DE OVERVAL until the early 1980s, when the print was deposited at the Nederlands Filmmuseum, provided more useful information. Gofilex's former director remembered that, whenever they wanted to distribute the 16mm copy, they had to contact Tuschinski for permission, and so a tentative conclusion emerged that the copyright of DE OVERVAL was indeed assigned from Sapphire to Tuschinski in 1973.

Assuming that this was true, the next step in trying to determine the film's current copyright holder was to discover whether the rights had been assigned once again in 1992, the year in which (after various name changes) Tuschinski was subsumed by Pathé, becoming the company's film rental department. The only person still working at Pathé who had also worked at Tuschinski was Pathé's archivist. She identified the person who dealt with the legal transactions in 1992 as Tuschinski's former financial director. However, the financial director in turn could not remember whether the company had owned the copyright to any of the Sapphire films or whether those rights had played any part in the merger transactions. Nor could the archivist find any certificate in Pathé's archive, which includes Tuschinski's company archive, that would prove that the rights had been assigned.

Thus, after several months of research, often based (of necessity) on assumptions, the key turning points in Sapphire's company history remained obscure, and there was no conclusive answer to the question of DE OVERVAL's current copyright ownership. Nevertheless, despite the lack of an identifiable and locatable copyright holder, the Nederlands Filmmuseum decided to go ahead with the film's production and distribution as a DVD. Its risk analysis covered the history of the film material's use and the potential risk of a rights holder coming forward after publication. Of course, a different archive might have made a different decision.

DE OVERVAL is an example of one problematic title in one particular archive. At the time of the research into the film's copyright, in 2003, there was no specific term for a film that was still in the period of copyright but lacking clear copyright ownership; now, such a film is called an 'orphan work' and the whole issue is known as the 'orphan works problem'. At the time of writing, nearly fifteen years after the film's DVD distribution, there is still no claim to this particular orphan work's copyright ownership.[5] Its case illustrates how the inability to clear the rights for such a film can significantly delay or even halt its distribution: as copyright law stands, reuse may be prevented if permission cannot be obtained (van Gompel, 2007a; 2007b; Elferink and Ringnalda, 2008). The DE OVERVAL story shows that tracing copyright owners is a time-consuming process, with no guarantee of success, and it is clearly not feasible for an archive to investigate the history of every individual orphan title it holds in the same exhaustive fashion.

THE 'ORPHAN WORKS PROBLEM' AND ITS CAUSES

Recategorizing film archival holdings based on copyright ownership reveals that orphan works are the films that raise the most problems in terms of public access. When films are still within the copyright period but the rights holder can be neither identified nor located, the archive is unable to seek permission to duplicate and disseminate them. As archives rarely use orphan works without permission, this has obvious ramifications: the potentially beneficial use of these films is severely hindered and much in the archival collection is condemned to lie dormant. This, in sum, is the 'orphan works problem'.

It is worth spending a moment here to revisit the orphan Jack – the 'handbag baby' we first encountered in the Introduction. The play in which he appears, *The Importance of Being Earnest,* could not only be used as an analogy for the individual orphan film, but also as a blueprint for the whole orphan works problem. Much of its comedy sprang from 'people behaving with such obsessive earnestness of purpose that they have lost all sense of proportion' (Cave, 2000, p. 430); with orphan works, if the law is followed to the letter, no one benefits – a truly disproportionate result given all the potential benefits of reusing the films.

In the case of the legally uncertain category of orphan films, the film archive is a sort of safety net or temporary 'placeholder' – or, if we extend the analogy with the play, a 'handbag'. Archives, especially public-sector ones, safeguard those films that, in the absence of a rights holder, have lost the commercial value that usually provides an incentive for preservation. However, when films cannot be reused legally, archivists sometimes still decide on their reuse, after undertaking a risk analysis. Thus, by resisting some of the copyright law's applications in this way, the archive plays an active role in shaping access to its holdings. This is especially important when the rights holders are not aware that they actually own the rights to a film; when it could be assumed they would not have objected to its reuse; or when there is a certain degree of plausibility to the conclusion that there are no rights holders left. The agency of the archivist, particularly vis-à-vis such potentially significant decisions, is a consistently under-researched component of archival access practices – one that is explored in more detail in this chapter and the next.

The orphan works problem is not new. The issue of unidentifiable or unlocatable copyright holders stretches further back in time than the recent interest in the phenomenon would suggest. That said, the problem has taken on a more urgent character in the last decade, particularly because the success of public archive funding applications is often predicated on the (online) dissemination of their holdings, and because of the rising number of aggregated initiatives to promote digital access to cultural heritage.

Definition, demarcation, and scope

There are two different, and not entirely compatible, definitions of an orphan work. The first is a strictly legal definition: 'a copyright protected work [...], the right owner(s) of which cannot be identified or located by someone who wants to make use of the work in a manner that requires the right owner's consent' (van Gompel, 2007a, p. 2).[6] The author expands the definition in a later article to claim that a situation in which the inability to acquire permission from the right owner(s) makes it 'impossible to reutilise the work legally' (van Gompel, 2007b, p. 670) – and this hints at the practical nature of the dilemma – is generally seen as the orphan works problem.

The latter is a more conceptual definition. According to film professor and Orphan Film Symposium[7] founder Dan Streible:

> [The definition should include] the curatorial and intellectual energy associated with the phenomenon. Orphan films can be conceived as all types of neglected cinema. While a film might not be literally abandoned by its owner, if it is unseen or not part of the universe of knowledge about moving images, it is essentially orphaned. Its orphan-ness might be material, conceptual, or both. Physical deterioration obviously puts films at risk. In this sense, more moving image works are orphaned – or headed to the orphanage – than not. But even a preserved and well-stored film is orphan-like if its existence is unknown outside of the archive. (Streible, 2009, p. x)

In contrast to the legal definition, this conceptual definition of an orphan work comprises all works that lack the 'commercial potential to pay for their continued preservation' (Melville and Simmon, 1993, p. xi). This includes all films outside the commercial mainstream and encompasses those works in the public domain.[8] Paulo Cherchi Usai (2009) has even extended this definition to argue that, in a digital context, all analogue films could be seen as orphan works.

Both definitions, however, highlight the fact that an orphan work is not a stable or fixed entity. Its 'orphanhood' – whether defined by copyright ownership or its commercial potential for preservation – can be lost or gained. For instance, a film loses its legal orphan status as soon as a copyright holder is identified and/or located, or the film is identified as public domain. Alternatively, a work can also *become* orphaned once the commercial incentive for its continued preservation is lacking. Due to the different definitions of orphan works, it is difficult to delineate the orphan works problem precisely. Even when adhering strictly to the legal definition, for example, demarcating the problem is difficult as the criteria for the terms 'unidentifiable' and 'un-locatable' are subjective. Recent developments have tried to tackle some of these issues in diligent search guidelines, which we will look at in the next part of this chapter.

This book, due to its specific focus, examines orphan works according to their legal definition. Arguably, orphan films and films in the public domain are equally marginalized and neglected as both lack the commercial potential that would guarantee their preservation, but public domain films, which should not pose any legal problems, form a separate category in the debate on copyright ownership and archival access. An archival recategorization, one that considers orphan films and public domain films separately, allows us to discern a wider network of factors relating to the problem of access, including those factors that have been systematically overlooked or underrepresented: human agency and contemporary economics. This is easier to do when orphan works are considered separately. The public domain films therefore comprise the topic of the next chapter.

According to a United States Copyright Office study (2006, p. 2) on orphan works, *Report on Orphan Works*, some of the obstacles to successfully identifying and locating copyright owners include:

(1) inadequate identifying information on a copy of the work itself;
(2) inadequate information about copyright ownership because of a change of ownership or a change in the circumstances of the owner;
(3) limitations of existing copyright ownership information sources; and
(4) difficulties researching copyright information.

The report concludes that the orphan works problem is 'real' while at the same time 'elusive to quantify and describe comprehensively' (p. 7). A follow-up publication in 2012, which focuses on orphan works and mass digitization, adds that the orphan works problem 'affects a broad cross section of stakeholders including members of the general public, archives, publishers and filmmakers' (Pallante, 2012b, p. 64555).

The large majority of films that are considered to be orphan works will be found in public archives. Commercial archives, such as studio archives, mostly house films with clear legal ownership and so include few or no 'true' orphan works. Sometimes, the rights to the play or novel on which a film is based belong to an external party, and the costs of renewing these underlying rights can be so prohibitive that the films end up 'lost' within the archive (Allen, 2010).[9] Films most at risk of becoming orphaned are 'newsreels, regional documentaries, avant-garde and independent productions, silent-era films, amateur works, and scientific and anthropological footage' (NFPF, 2004, p. 3). Commercially produced films by production companies that have gone out of business or transferred their rights to another entity can be added to this list (NFPF, 2004; HLG, 2008).

Some of the early estimations of the scope of the orphan works problem ranged from 40% at the British Library to '58% of all holdings' at Cornell University Library (Elferink and Ringnalda, 2008, p. 25). Recent estimates by several European audiovisual archives of the number of their orphan works range from 5% to 21% of all holdings – these were the percentages put forward by the representatives of EYE and the Danish Film Institute, respectively, at the EFG 'Taking Care of Orphan Works' conference in May 2011 in Amsterdam.[10] And again, this range can be explained by the different definitions of orphan works, as well as the level of research. The estimates rested on a first appraisal, but more research would be necessary to determine the legal status of an archival holding more precisely.

In the context of the large-scale Dutch digitization project, 'Images for the Future,'[11] EYE mapped the legal status of its film collections, with a specific focus on orphan works. In her conference presentation, the institute's legal project officer, Géraldine Vooren, detailed her findings: out of the 40,000 titles in EYE's film collection, some 1,800 titles were identified as orphan films. Vooren also listed, in descending order, the specific reasons why the works in question were considered to be orphan. Reason one was 'unknown authors', which applied mostly to documentaries, amateur films, and newsreels; the second reason was 'unidentified heirs'; the third comprised 'production companies that had ceased to exist'; and the fourth was 'identified, but untraceable authors'. At times, there is no knowledge of who made a work. This happens in cases in which there are, for instance, no (more) credits on a film, so it is difficult to determine whether it is within the period of copyright. At other times, although it can be determined that a film is still in copyright, it is difficult to establish who currently owns the rights. The case of DE OVER-VAL highlighted above exemplifies this problem. And sometimes, even when there is an identified rights holder, they cannot be located. So, in the rather optimistic assessment of one national archive, it means that roughly 5% of the institution's entire film collection could be considered orphan films.[12]

To provide some context for what these numbers mean, it is worth considering the survival rate of silent films. Cherchi Usai (1996), Vinzenz Hediger (2005), and Thomas Christensen (2017) have estimated that only around 15-20% of worldwide silent film production survives in the archives today, and Jan-Christopher Horak (2007, p. 29) claims that we know 'as much about silent cinema as we do about ancient Greek pottery'. The amount of silent film material that is left forms the basis of our entire understanding of that period of film history. Estimates of how many film works are currently dormant because of their orphaned status could, in the worst-case scenario, correspond to roughly the same amount. The consequences of these numbers for the material's potential for 'history making' seem undeniable in a time in which ubiquitous access is the norm.

Legal causes

So how did we end up with an orphan works problem? The legal and administrative causes that underlie the problem comprise the warp and weft of a larger network of factors, no single one of which is the sole reason. The most important legal causes of orphan works are threefold. First, the term of copyright lasts a long time: it not only takes a long time before the work enters the public domain, when it can be reused without permission, but there is also a fair chance that information about copyright ownership will go missing over this period. Second, there is no complete record of what belongs to whom. This is partially due to the elimination of the mandatory requirement for copyright formalities. Although it is true that, even when these formalities were in place, the records were not necessarily complete or up-to-date, their existence did potentially provide a clearer starting point from which to launch a search for the rights holder. And third, multiple individuals determine the duration of the term of a copyright, which complicates the search for information. This situation is even more complex in the case of film copyright as these individuals will differ from country to country, and there are also many possible copyright owners, which muddies the waters when trying to establish a clear chain of ownership.[13] Here, we consider each of these factors in more detail.

1. EXTENSION OF THE COPYRIGHT TERM

In 1995, the European Union's Copyright Duration Directive (93/98/EEC) extended the copyright protection term among its Member States. 'Life of the author plus 50 years' became 'life of the author plus 70 years'. The US also extended the term in 1998, but its Copyright Term Extension Act only applied to those works still in copyright. By contrast, the EU retroactively revived the term of some works that had already fallen out of copyright by the time of the Directive's passage. This applied to a large number of works that were in or would soon enter the public domain. As a result, there were even fewer works freely available than before. In his 2004 publication, *Free Culture*, Lawrence Lessig explains some of the consequences of the term extension:

> It is valuable copyrights that are responsible for terms being extended. Mickey Mouse and 'Rhapsody in Blue.' These works are too valuable for copyright owners to ignore. But the real harm to our society from copyright extensions is not that Mickey Mouse remains Disney's. Forget Mickey Mouse. Forget Robert Frost. Forget all the works from the 1920s and 1930s that have continuing commercial value. The real harm of term extension comes not from these famous works. The real harm is to the works that are not famous, not commercially exploited, and no longer available as a result. [...] Of all the creative work produced by humans everywhere, a tiny fraction has continuing commercial value. For that tiny fraction, the copyright is a crucially important legal device. For that tiny fraction, the copyright creates incentives to produce and distribute the creative work. (Lessig, 2004, pp. 221-225)

Currently, works are in copyright for the longest period of time since the inception of copyright legislation. Lessig (2001; 2004; 2008), one of the most prolific protagonists of the so-called 'free culture movement' of the mid noughties, vehemently opposed the extension and advocated a return to a much shorter term.[14] He argued in numerous publications that due to the extension – and revival – of copyright terms, a whole generation of works had been forced into lockdown. Fewer works now enter the public domain, where they can be reused without restrictions.

The extension of the term of copyright protection, however, may appear to simplify the situation in the film world – in the UK, for example, copyright in some films expired 50 years from the end of the year in which it was made, so extending copyright to life plus 70 years is an incredibly impactful change.[15] But, for film archives (and for many general archives), a longer copyright term mainly means it will be even harder to trace the information needed to clarify ownership. More works in copyright implies that the archive will need to trace even more owners to ask for permission to reuse their works. This is a time-consuming and costly process, particularly in relation to older works, and will not necessarily be successful – as the earlier example of DE OVERVAL demonstrated. Taking into account differences on a national level (the UK government, for instance, has recently introduced a licensing scheme for orphan works, which is discussed in more detail later), if the search is unsuccessful, permission to reuse the work can be withheld. Partially depending on the archivists' cooperation, the potential user of the material has two choices: they can go ahead with the project regardless and bear the risk of an infringement claim, or they can abandon it entirely, rendering the work and its potentially productive and beneficial uses redundant. Recent developments have also tried to tackle some of these issues, which we will look at in the next part of this chapter.

2. ELIMINATION OF MANDATORY COPYRIGHT FORMALITIES

Copyright is currently considered to 'come into existence from the point of creation' (Deazley, 2006, p. 102). At one time, however, there were mandatory registration formalities:

> Formalities as a requirement for protection were abolished with the 1908 Berlin revision of the Berne Convention and were in turn gradually eliminated in all the signatory countries. [...] This has resulted, in many cases, in a lack of sufficient or adequate identifying information. Because of the elimination of formalities, the number of orphan works has increased, most notably because some works may not bear a signature or other imprint of the author's identity. (Borghi and Karapapa, 2013, pp. 73-74)

Different countries had different kinds of formalities – for example, affixing a copyright notice to the work itself. The US did not abandon formalities as a prerequisite for protection until it joined the Berne Convention in 1989 (van Gompel, 2011). In fact, mandatory copyright formalities were instrumental in preserving the earliest chapter in US film, which might otherwise have been lost to history (Chapter 6 looks at this situation in more detail).

The past decade, however, has seen calls for a reintroduction of mandatory copyright formalities, partially to deal with problems relating to the digital realm. Digitization has resulted in a decentralization of the production, access, and consumption of works. Material can be reused relatively easily by almost everyone on a potentially (online) global scale. Stef van Gompel (2011) has investigated whether a reintroduction of copyright formalities is legally feasible, arguing that the main reasons behind abolishing mandatory formalities in the course of the 20th century were predominantly pragmatic, although there were other more ideological motives. More importantly, however, he argues that these historical rationales for abolishing copyright formalities have largely disappeared in today's digital era.

A reintroduction of mandatory formalities could have far-reaching consequences for archival collections. It could, for instance, lead to a more comprehensive central record of legal metadata, which would improve future copyright clearance processes. It would not necessarily lead to conclusive ownership information later on in an artwork's life cycle, but it would very likely provide a clearer point from which to start tracking down that information.[16]

A discussion around reintroducing mandatory formalities remains beyond the scope of this book, particularly as it is more complex than the simple cause-and-effect reason that it would lead to more complete and up-to-date legal metadata. Consider, for instance, the legal deposit of audiovisual works:

> [S]tructured and organised deposit of cinematographic elements exists in almost all [EU] MS [Member States]. These take the form of legal deposit (in 11 MS) or of compulsory, contractually-bound deposit for publicly funded films (in 16 MS). Only the Netherlands and the UK rely almost exclusively on voluntary deposit (the UK has an exception for the films co-financed with Lottery funds). Very few countries, such as France, require the deposit of all movies distributed in the country. (Mazzanti, 2011, p. 48).

On the one hand, legal deposit creates both a centralized record of information and a centralized record of material holdings. Yet, those countries with legal deposit do not have a smaller orphan works problem, as a representative of the Danish Film Archive at the 'Taking Care of Orphan Works' conference illustrated:[17] having to deposit and register works initially does not necessarily lead to clear ownership information later on. Again, however, this is not to say that legal deposit could not help towards a more comprehensive central record of legal metadata, which would improve future copyright clearance processes. It is certainly easier to collect a copy of a work when it is first distributed, as opposed to later.

On the other hand, the deposit is often linked to a specific funding scheme, so, in practice, it is difficult to get a copy of *every* film produced (the system is also usually inapplicable to foreign works, which are arguably also important to collect in light of a national film culture). Moreover, legal deposit can also have far-reaching consequences for the quality of the work deposited. When a second- or third-generation copy of a work is deposited in an archive, in order to comply with legal formalities, it will be these copies that become (for potential lack of better material) the source material for the work's restoration in the future. A particularly current issue is that many archives are accepting digital-born materials, but, as there is not yet a universal standardization of this process, these potential sources are of vastly diverging quality (Fossati, 2009; Heller and Flueckiger, 2017).

3. MULTIPLE INDIVIDUALS DETERMINING COPYRIGHT EXPIRATION

The term of copyright in a film is based on the life span of multiple individuals. In the UK, for instance:

> [Copyright duration is] calculated in accordance with the last to die of four designated persons: the director, the author of the screenplay, the author of the film dialogue (if different), and the composer of any specifically created film score. [...] [T]hese are only relevant lives for calculating duration of protection. They are not deemed to be the authors of the film. Rather, the CDPA defines the author of a film as 'the producer and the principal director'. (Deazley, 2017, C6, p. 13)

At the time of writing, a film is in the public domain if all of these individuals died before 1948; if any of them died after 1948, that film is in copyright. Even if there is no information available for any of these figures, the film could still be within the period of copyright. The larger the number of individuals involved, the greater the amount of research needed to determine whether a film is still in copyright.[18] Moreover, these individuals can differ from the current rights holders. As stated earlier, the duration of film copyright is particularly complicated, so recreating a chain of title can require substantive investigation.

Copyright term extension, elimination of mandatory copyright formalities, and multiple individuals determining copyright expiration are some of the legal causes underlying the orphan works problem that impact archival practice directly. However, archival practice in turn harbours its own administrative causes to the orphan works problem.

Administrative causes

The legal causes of the orphan works problem are interwoven with a set of more administrative (and political) causes. These include 1) unclear archival origins of (parts of) an archive's collection; 2) a lack of identifying information about the works themselves; and 3) a structural lack of the necessary manpower and financial infrastructure in public-sector archives to enable them to undertake research on a title-by-title basis. The following section looks at these factors in more detail.

1. UNCLEAR ARCHIVAL ORIGINS
Public-sector film archives comprise national archives – generally large institutions – which safeguard a substantial part of a country's audiovisual heritage; broadcasting archives, which safeguard a selection of radio and/or audiovisual programmes and sometimes operate under the auspices of a broadcasting company; and regional and local archives, which generally adhere to a more or less thematic curatorial approach. Donations or deposits to these archives can come in large quantities, and the origins of older parts of their collections in particular are often opaque. In terms of their legal metadata, most public-sector archives find themselves in a comparable situation: their records are incomplete and out-of-date. This has obvious implications for locating copyright owners at a later stage.

2. LACK OF IDENTIFYING INFORMATION ON THE WORKS THEMSELVES
Previous chapters have shown that the idea of the film archive as a place full of pristine film copies, simply waiting to be discovered, is a myth. The reality is that many archival films are incomplete (Delpeut, 1997). It is not unusual for a work to lack even the most basic information, such as the names of its creators in the opening or closing credits, and if there are additional documents relating to the film; more often than not, they also fail to reveal this information. Certain works, such as documentaries, avant-garde productions, silent-era films, and anthropological footage, are at higher risk of being orphaned, given the instability of the producers of those kinds of materials over time. The lack of identifying information accompanying these films makes it hard even to begin, far less to sustain, a search for potential rights holders. Even in

cases in which some of the names of those connected to the film are known, their contact information is frequently out-of-date. Even when a search is potentially feasible because, for instance, the name of the original production company is known, it often turns out that the company has ceased to exist and it is unclear what happened to the material and intellectual property rights of the film.

3. STRUCTURAL PROBLEMS: LACK OF MANPOWER AND FINANCIAL INFRASTRUCTURE

Donations or deposits to a public-sector archive can consist of large volumes and there is often not enough expert staff on hand to identify and catalogue the material immediately and comprehensively. This staff issue creates a backlog that has obvious consequences at a later stage. Only a team of full-time employees working daily on the search for copyright owners, such as the legal team that EYE fielded at the height of its large national digitization project 'Images for the Future', could have led to what EYE claims to be one of the lowest percentages of orphan works recorded within a public-sector film archive.

The legal and administrative causes that underlie the orphan works problem are interlinked. Some of the underlying legal causes without doubt have far-reaching consequences for the later archival work, but they are frequently exacerbated by the administrative and bureaucratic causes that originate in the archival practice itself. The most important consequence of this complex network of factors is an incomplete record of legal metadata. Tracing or contacting rights owners for permission is difficult and, as a consequence, the distribution of audiovisual archival material is often significantly delayed or put on hold indefinitely.

As van Gompel and Bernt Hugenholtz (2010) argue, the orphan works problem can be seen as one of *information*. The problem need not exist, and, when it does, it need not progress. In archival practice, however, it seems that works with 'copyright issues' have a tendency to move down the queue of works to be preserved – especially if there is a funding obligation to make the work (digitally) available. But, as long as there is enough manpower and willpower (as well as the financial infrastructure) to do the necessary research, the legal status of a work can be determined.

Thus, the incompleteness of the legal metadata brings to light the fact that the orphan works problem is not an exclusively legal one; it is intimately related to archival practice. Furthermore, it reveals a history of film in which the record is always necessarily fragmented, an issue to which Chapters 5 and 6 will return.

PROPOSED SOLUTIONS TO THE ORPHAN WORKS PROBLEM

As with the causes, the legal and administrative measures underlying some of the solutions to the orphan works problem also comprise a complex network, which includes the efforts of legislating bodies, academia, and archivists, as well as collective organizations in the film sector. Each influences the other reciprocally.

Orphan works first began to gain prominence in the literature about a decade ago. Initially, the focus was on identifying and mapping the problem, but interest rapidly shifted to what it meant in light of the push for mass digitization, and equally as quickly, the term 'orphan works' made its way into general IP textbooks.

Meanwhile, film archival practice instituted a version of what would now be called a 'diligent search' in order to keep their collections workable, which helped shape the legal diligent search guidelines. The recent legislation has in turn impacted archival practice, changing what archives can and cannot lawfully do with orphan works, with far-reaching consequences for their daily practices of preservation, access, digital reproduction, and general services to the public. We are currently very much *in medias res* and we will have to see how some of these issues will pan out.

Legislative measures

In the UK, there were two specific attempts to address the orphan works issue prior to the introduction of the Orphan Works Directive in 2012. The first was the *Gowers Review of Intellectual Property* in 2006. This was a study commissioned by the British government to review a proposal to extend the term of copyright protection (for recorded music) from 50 years to 95 years (both retroactively and prospectively), including a provision for orphan works that would amend the Copyright Directive 2001/29/EC. The review concluded that the extension was not supported by the economic analysis of its effects (Library of Congress, 2010). The second review, in 2011, the *Hargreaves Review of Intellectual Property and Growth*, noted that the 'problem of orphan works – works to which access is effectively barred because the copyright holder cannot be traced – represents the starkest failure of the copyright framework to adapt. The copyright system is locking away millions of works in this category' (p. 38). It recommended that the 'government should legislate to enable licensing of orphan works' (p. 40).[19]

Designing a legal solution to regulate the use of orphan works is certainly not easy: the legislation has to promote creativity and innovation by allowing the material to be put to new uses, but, at the same time, protect the interests of any potential copyright owners (Mendis, 2016). For this reason, any legislation will face a whole range of issues. For example, it has to include a comprehensive definition of orphan works, draw up adequate due diligence guidelines, and establish a regulatory body, as well as include remuneration schemes with precisely defined moments of payment, be it at the time of the actual reuse of the material or at the time of the rights owner's potential claim. It also has to address the fact that the kind of permitted uses (educational, commercial, and so on), which ideally should apply to all uses and all users, need to accord with previous directives and international conventions. The legislation has to function effectively as part of an international framework that encompasses many different legal traditions.[20]

THE ORPHAN WORKS DIRECTIVE

The resulting legal solution was the Orphan Works Directive 2012/28/EU. The Directive prescribed that EU Member States should introduce a new exception to copyright for certain permitted uses of orphan works, and this should be incorporated into national law by October 2014. Many Member States have implemented the Directive, adopting a limited number of variations to the subjective and objective scope and permitted uses of orphan works. Here, we focus mainly on the Netherlands and the UK.

The Netherlands has implemented the Directive as an exception to the copyright rule for cultural and heritage organizations. This exception allows these organizations to digitize their orphan works and make them available online for noncommercial purposes, after conducting a diligent search. The legislation provides a list of specific sources that the heritage institution should consult in its attempt to locate the rights holder, as well as general indications on how to locate other sources, such as collecting societies and authors' guilds. Different countries, however, use orphan works in different ways, whether it be preservation, education, or 'digital' publication (Favale et al., 2016). EYE, for example, has interpreted the text of the Orphan Works Directive as also including commercial reuse (Bout, 2017), which will be further discussed in the next section.

The Orphan Works Directive requires that an archive carry out a diligent search for rights holders before a work is declared an orphan and falls into the exemption category. In general, the diligent search has to be carried out in the Member State where the work was first published, except in the case of an audiovisual work, when it must be carried out in the Member State that is home to the producer's headquarters or their habitual residence. The Directive leaves the choice about what sources should be consulted to meet the requirements of a diligent search up to the individual Member State, and many are now in the process of issuing lists of sources (Bertoni et al., 2017). The number of sources, and their appropriateness, however, varies considerably between Member States: The Netherlands, for instance, has produced a list of 45 for an audiovisual work in contrast to 72 in Italy (Favale et al., 2016).

The approach to a solution in the UK is, in some senses, unique:

> [It has] adopted a twin-track solution to the orphan works problem in the form of an exception based on the Orphan Works Directive and an Orphan Works Licensing Scheme (OWLS). Both the exception and the licensing scheme turn on carrying out a diligent search for the owner(s) of the copyright in the work. While the orphan works regime may have value for small-scale digitisation initiatives, the mandatory nature of this diligent search requirement means the regime is largely irrelevant for mass digitisation schemes. Put another way, mass digitisation and diligent search are fundamentally incompatible. (Deazley, 2017, C9, p. 2)[21]

There are clear differences between the two systems: OWLS is much broader in scope than the European Directive as it applies to all types of copyright work and anyone can apply for a licence, not just certain institutions, as mandated by the Directive. Perhaps even more importantly, it enables both commercial and noncommercial uses of orphan works (Deazley, 2017, C9). The licences, however, are capped at seven years; after this time, a new diligent search is required and a new licence application must be filed at the Orphan Works Register.[22] In summary:

> [W]hereas the Directive enables the use of certain orphan works by certain organisations for certain purposes (across the EU), OWLS enables the use of *all orphan works by [almost] anyone for any purpose* (but only within the UK). (Deazley, 2017, C9, p. 9)

Sometimes, the choice between the two systems might not be all that clear. If a film archive is interested in digitizing a film and providing online access, the option of applying for a new licence every seven years might not be particularly attractive; however, the exception under the Directive is currently limited to noncommercial use only. Both systems hinge on a diligent search, and the ramifications of this are becoming increasingly noticeable in archival practice. The requirements for the diligent search can lead to extreme situations in which – as a representative of the British Film Institute at the 2015 'Colour Fantastic' conference in Amsterdam jokingly remarked – archivists have to instigate a search for the fourth-generation heirs of Victorian filmmakers whom they are certain will never be traced.

Moreover, research on a pan-European level has revealed that a sizeable number of the sources that archivists are required to consult in order to locate rights holders are not freely available online: general repositories and data-bases are accessible, but authors' guilds and unions generally are not, while newspaper archives often charge a fee (Favale et al., 2016). As a result, it is not evident how a cultural institution can clear the rights of its collections if it fully complies with all the legislative requirements:

> It emerges that the effectiveness of the Directive in fostering harmonisa-tion within the internal market and mass-digitisation processes is rather limited by, primarily, the unsustainability of the Diligent Search. The Diligent Search highly depends on the number of sources that need to be consulted and their accessibility. As long as there is no hierarchical validity of sources by law and not all sources are freely accessible online, it remains unclear how the clearing of rights will happen in order to fully comply with the requirements of each legislation. (Bertoni et al., 2017)[23]

We are currently in the midst of the rollout of the implementation of the Orphan Works Directive and will have to wait to see how some of these issues will pan out over the next few years.

Administrative measures

Prior to the recent legislation, one of the most pragmatic ways of dealing with the orphan works problem was to employ a team of (legal) staff to research the historical and current status of the archival film to determine whether it was in copyright, and, if so, whether it had an identifiable and locatable rights holder. If it was determined that there was no rights holder, the work could be labelled as a public domain film, and, if a rights holder existed, further research would include establishing up-to-date contact information so that the archive could seek permission to use the film (and a transaction could take place between the rights holder and the 'good faith user').[24] As the case of DE OVERVAL has shown, if the search for a rights holder was unsuccessful, the archive could decide whether to go ahead and make the work available. Before doing so, it would undertake a risk assessment (in some ways, a precursor of the diligent search), which would involve proving that everything possible had been done to find the potential rights holder and gauging the probability that one might come forward after the reuse. Following this assessment, sometimes the archive would take the risk; sometimes, not.

In the lead-up to the legislation, there were also a few experiments with databases that depend on voluntary registration – a so-called 'opt-in' scenario. The obvious drawback of this for orphan works is that the rights holders who sign up will already be aware of their property.[25] However, part of the orphan works problem is that some of the rights holders might be missing or ignorant of their rights, so a database with voluntary registration does not seem to be an exhaustive resolution.[26]

As the Introduction argues, the rules of the IP system are not and cannot be applied mechanically; rather, they are 'activated' in and by their specific context. This is reflected in the pragmatic approach that EYE takes to the diligent search criteria, based on the understanding that highly experienced archivists are free to exercise a certain professional discretion. This means that sources are only consulted if they are relevant – even if they are legally mandatory. In some cases, it means not consulting *any* sources (Bout, 2017).

The same pragmatic approach can be seen in the interpretation of the possible uses of orphan works, which EYE has interpreted as including 'commercial' reuse. The fee that EYE charges third parties when making material available represents a reimbursement for the storage, preservation, digitization, and other costs incurred by the institute. Strictly speaking, this practice generates income (although not any profit), a practice that both the Orphan Works Directive and the Dutch Copyright Act allow, as long as the revenues are used for digitizing and making available (yet more) orphan works:

> The organisations referred to in Article 1(1) [publicly accessible libraries, educational establishments and museums, as well as [...] archives, film or audio heritage institutions and public-service broadcasting organisations, established in the Member States] shall use an orphan work in accordance with paragraph 1 [(a) making the orphan work available to the public; (b) by acts of reproduction [...] for the purposes of digitisation, making available, indexing, cataloguing, preservation or restoration] only in order to achieve aims related to their public-interest missions, in particular the preservation of, the restoration of, and the provision of cultural and educational access to, works and phonograms contained in their collection. The organisations may generate revenues in the course of such uses, for the exclusive purpose of covering their costs of digitising orphan works and making them available to the public. (OWD, Art. 6(2))[27]

EYE puts all its sales revenues towards preservation, and because the mission laid down in its founding statutes includes the remit to provide third parties with material from its collection, it considers itself compliant with the Directive (Bout, 2017).[28]

If EYE undertook research into the rights holders of DE OVERVAL today, it would trace the most appropriate sources on the list of diligent search sources. At some point (far sooner than it took 15 years ago), it would declare the film a 'certified' orphan. The title would be uploaded to the orphan works database of the European Intellectual Property Office (EUIPO),[29] which, in turn, would send it to the Dutch national authority, the Rijksdienst voor Cultureel Erfgoed (Cultural Heritage Agency of the Netherlands), for authorization. This information would then be available for cross-border use within the EU Member States,[30] which means that, if someone in one of the other Member States wanted to make use of the film, they would not have to replicate the research.

This chapter has examined some of the causes of and proposed solutions to the orphan works problem in light of its potential historiographic repercussions. The problem should not be understood exclusively as the effect of a specific legal discourse, but needs to be seen as part of a more complex issue: intellectual property *in relation to* archival practices and administrative procedures – that is, 'intellectual property as a bureaucratic reality' (Bellido, 2014, p. 15). In order to unravel some of the contemporary aspects of this process, the next chapter will focus on those works that are free from legal restrictions, the films in quadrants 3 and 4 – that is, works in the public domain.

NOTES

1   This is an 'unofficial' translation by Mireille van Eechoud, professor of Information Law at the University of Amsterdam. The translation has been published as an annex in Bernt Hugenholtz et al. (2012) and is available at: https://www.ivir.nl/syscontent/pdfs/119.pdf (accessed on 9 October 2017). The translation is called 'unofficial' because Dutch laws are established in the Dutch language only and therefore the translated document is not legally binding. This information was provided by Dutch legislative expert Just van der Hoeven in an email to the author on 10 March 2015.

2   The film's director, Paul Rotha, died in 1984; Else van Epen-de Groot, who created the music for the film work, died in 1994; screenwriter Louis de Jong died in 2005; and Kees Brusse, one of the main actors in the film but also the dialogue director (and who could therefore perhaps be considered a codirector), died in 2013.

3   Amsterdam Chamber of Commerce, dossier number: 33097271.

4   This is 'shocking' information in itself, as this would mean that FANFARE, arguably one of the most famous Dutch feature films, would be an orphan work.

5   EYE Film Institute Netherlands has *never* had any cases in which previously unidentified and un-located copyright holders have come forward after a film has

been made public. This information was provided by Ronny Temme (former head of sales at EYE) in an email to the author on 10 May 2010.

6   This is a variation on the 2006 *Report on Orphan Works*, in which the US Copyright Office defines orphan works as 'a term used to describe the situation where the owner of a copyrighted work cannot be identified and located by someone who wishes to make use of the work in a manner that requires permission of the copyright owner' (p. 1).

7   A biannual film symposium that solicits presentations about preserving, studying, and reusing orphan works. For more information, see: http://www.nyu. edu/orphanfilm/.

8   Incidentally, this is also the opinion of Jack Valenti, former president of the Motion Picture Association of America. Valenti (cited in Netanel, 2008, p. 200) thought that 'the true orphan works problem arises from copyright's absence, not the great difficulty in locating the copyright holder: "A public domain work is an orphan. No one is responsible for its life [...] it becomes soiled and haggard."'

9   Another example would be the re-clearing of the rights for a specific actor for a disproportionate renewal fee. Due to contractual reasons, this can be so prohibitive that the production does not get rebroadcast. This information was provided by Claudio Ricci, technical expert for film and series, Swiss Radio and Television, in a personal conversation, 29 July 2014.

10 A 2010 orphan works survey, executed by the Association of European Cinémathèques (ACE) held that a little over 20% of audiovisual works in 24 European film heritage institutions were deemed to be orphan. For more details, see ACE (2010).

11 Consortium partners included EYE Film Institute Netherlands, the Netherlands Institute for Sound and Vision, the Dutch National Archives, and Kennisland. For more information, see: http://imagesforthefuture.com/en/.

12 In a more recent estimate based on a database search in September 2017, the percentage is approximately the same. See Chapter 1 for more information.

13 For a wonderful explanation of just how difficult the duration of film copyright is in the UK, see Chapter 6 of 'Copyright 101', 'Copyright and Digital Cultural Heritage: Duration of Protection', at the online resource the Copyright Cortex. Available at: https://copyrightcortex.org/files/copyright101/6-CDCH-Duration-of-Protection.pdf (accessed on 10 October 2017).

14 In an op-ed piece in the *New York Times*, 20 May 2008, entitled 'Little Orphan Artworks', Lawrence Lessig describes his proposed solution as follows: 'Following the model of patent law, Congress should require a copyright owner to register a work after an initial and generous term of automatic and full protection. For 14 years, a copyright owner would need to do nothing to receive the full protection of copyright law. But after 14 years, to receive full protection, the owner would have to take the minimal step of registering the work with an approved, privately managed and competitive registry, and of paying the copyright office $1.'

15 For more information about copyright duration in films, see Chapter 6 of 'Copyright 101', 'Copyright and Digital Cultural Heritage: Duration of Copyright', at the online resource, the Copyright Cortex. Available at: https://copyrightcortex. org/files/copyright101/6-CDCH-Duration-of-Protection.pdf (accessed 9 October 2017).

16 Copyright in the US, for instance, is administered by the Library of Congress: a copyright search can be done at any time and, if the film's copyright was registered and renewed, that information is accessible. However, not all films were registered (Fishman, 2017).

17 Denmark has had a legal deposit scheme in place since the mid 1960s (Fossati, 2009). For a more detailed discussion on legal deposit, see Sabina Gorini (2004).

18 For more information about copyright duration in films, see Chapter 6 of 'Copyright 101', 'Copyright and Digital Cultural Heritage: Duration of Copyright', at the online resource, the Copyright Cortex. Available at: https://copyrightcortex. org/files/copyright101/6-CDCH-Duration-of-Protection.pdf (accessed 9 October 2017).

19 In the US, in the meantime, 'Congress came very close to adopting a consensus bill shortly before the presidential election in 2008, but did not enact orphan works legislation before adjourning' (Pallante, 2012b, p. 64556).

20 'In the EU, it is a prerequisite that all Member States have solutions, which are interoperable and agree to mutually recognise any mechanism that fulfils the generally accepted core principles. Mutual recognition is important with a view to the cross-border nature of the use.' (HLG, 2008, p. 5)

21 For an excellent discussion of the orphan works problem, including the advantages and disadvantages of the proposed solutions, see the rest of Chapter 9 of 'Copyright 101', 'Copyright and Digital Cultural Heritage: Orphan Works', at the online resource the Copyright Cortex. Available at: https://copyrightcortex.org/ files/copyright101/9-CDCH-Orphan-Works.pdf (accessed on 11 October 2017).

22 There are currently six results in the category 'moving images' of the Orphan Works Register. Available at: https://www.orphanworkslicensing.service.gov.uk/ view-register/search?workCategory=All&filter=0 (accessed on 12 October 2017).

23 Some have even suggested that using Blockchain (the leading software platform for digital assets) as a registration system for the diligent search would be the solution to the orphan works problem (Hunter, 2017).

24 EYE acknowledges that these are some of the often-overlooked positive side effects of the diligent search: the public domain films that are unearthed in the process (for which no further rights clearance is necessary) and the identification of rights holders with whom agreements can be negotiated (Bout, 2017).

25 Although both are primarily geared towards the literary world, two examples of databases based on voluntary registration are ARROW and WATCH. ARROW (Accessible Registries of Rights Information and Orphan Works) was a project

undertaken by a consortium of European national libraries, publishers, collective management organizations, and writers (represented by their main European associations and a number of national organizations) that was launched in November 2008 and lasted for 30 months. Available at: http://www.arrow-net.eu/faq/what-arrow.html (accessed on 11 May 2013). WATCH is a database of copyright contacts for writers, artists, and prominent members of other creative fields. It is a joint project of the Harry Ransom Center (the University of Texas at Austin) and the University of Reading Library in the UK. Founded in 1994 as a resource for copyright questions about literary manuscripts held in the US and the UK, it has grown into one of the largest databases of copyright holders in the world. Available at: http://norman.hrc.utexas.edu/watch/about.cfm (accessed on 12 April 2016).

26   Under the Berne Convention, it is prohibited to 'establish mandatory registration systems or to mandate a copyright notice, including information on the identity and whereabouts of a copyright owner and the date of copyright, on each copy of the work. On the other hand, it is not prohibited to establish measures that stimulate rights owners to voluntarily provide information concerning copyright ownership and licensing conditions' (van Gompel and Hugenholtz, 2010, p. 4).

27   The full text of the Orphan Works Directive is available at: http://eur-lex.europa.eu/LexUriServ/LexUriServ.do?uri=OJ:L:2012:299:0005:0012:EN:PDF (accessed on 12 October 2017).

28   OWD, Art. 6(1) also lists the permitted uses, which include making the orphan work available to the public, within the meaning of Article 3 of Directive 2001/29/EC. This states: 'Member States shall provide authors with the exclusive right to authorise or prohibit any communication to the public of their works, by wire or wireless means, including the making available to the public of their works in such a way that members of the public may access them from a place and at a time individually chosen by them.' Leontien Bout (2017), legal counsel to EYE, argues that there is room to argue for a broad interpretation, as only the following part was transposed into Dutch law: 'the making available to the public of their works in such a way that members of the public may access them from a place and at a time individually chosen by them'. In addition, she argues that OWD, Art. 6(2) states that orphan works may only be used 'in order to achieve aims related to their [the organisations referred to in Art. 1(1)] public-interest missions'. OWD, Art. 6(2) suggests 'in *particular* the preservation of, the restoration of, and the provision of cultural and educational access to, works and phonograms contained in their collection'. This should not pose any problems in the case of EYE, since it is the institution's mission (as described in its foundation statutes) to provide third parties with material from its collection.

29   Available at: https://euipo.europa.eu/ohimportal/en/web/observatory/orphan-works-database (accessed on 12 October 2017).

30 This information is kept 'indefinitely', until either a rights holder comes forward (which, to this day, has not happened), until someone provides information why the particular title is not an orphan anymore, or until the work enters the public domain. EYE is one of the only archives that uses this method to register its orphan works. Other archives, particularly those that have interpreted the permitted uses in the OWD as quite narrow, see the registration of their orphan works as a limitation on their possibilities to reuse the works. Examples are the Belgian and the Polish film archives.

BIBLIOGRAPHY

Allen, Barry ([retired] Executive Director of Broadcast Services and Film Preservation, Paramount Pictures) (2010) Interviewed by Claudy Op den Kamp. Philadelphia, US, 4 November.

Bellido, José (2014) 'Howe and Griffiths' Concepts of Property in Intellectual Property', *Birkbeck Law Review*, 2(1), pp. 147–156.

Bertoni, Aura, Flavia Guerrieri, and Maria Lillà Montagnani (2017) *Report 2. Requirements for Diligent Search in 20 European Countries*. Bournemouth: EnDOW. Available at: http://diligentsearch.eu/wp-content/uploads/2017/06/REPORT-2.pdf (accessed on 11 October 2017).

Borghi, Maurizio, and Stavroula Karapapa (2013) *Copyright and Mass Digitization. A Cross-Jurisdictional Perspective*. Oxford: Oxford University Press.

Bout, Leontien (2017) 'Dealing with Orphan Works, a Dutch Film Archive's Perspective', EnDOW publication. Available at: http://diligentsearch.eu/wp-content/uploads/2017/11/L-Bout-presentation-orphan-works-a-film-archives-perspective.pdf (accessed on 9 November 2017).

Cave, Richard Allen (ed.) (2000) *The Importance of Being Earnest, and Other Plays*. London: Penguin Classics.

Cherchi Usai, Paolo (1996) 'The Early Years. Origins and Survival', in: Geoffrey Nowell-Smith (ed.) *The Oxford History of World Cinema*. Oxford: Oxford University Press, pp. 6-12.

Cherchi Usai, Paolo (2009) 'Are All (Analog) Films "Orphans"? A Pre-digital Appraisal', *The Moving Image*, 9(1), pp. 1–18.

Christensen, Thomas (2017) ' How to Destroy Film Heritage', *fi:re Film Restoration Summit*, Polish Film Institute, 9-10 November.

Deazley, Ronan (2006) *Rethinking Copyright: History, Theory, Language*. Northampton: Edward Elgar.

Deazley, Ronan (2017) 'Copyright 101', *Copyright Cortex* [online] available at: https://copyrightcortex.org/copyright-101 (accessed on 25 September 2017).

Delpeut, Peter (1997) *Cinéma Perdu. De eerste dertig jaar van de film 1895-1925*. Amsterdam: Uitgeverij Bas Lubberhuizen.

Elferink, Mirjam and Allard Ringnalda (2008) *Digitale Ontsluiting van Historische Archieven en Verweesde Werken: Een Inventarisatie*. Utrecht: CIER [Online]. Available at: http://www.wodc.nl/onderzoeksdatabase/ontsluiting-historische-archieven-en-auteursrecht-hoe-beter.aspx?cp=44&cs=6796 (accessed on 21 April 2016).

Favale, Marcella, Simone Schroff, and Aura Bertoni (2016) *Report 1. Requirements for Diligent Search in the United Kingdom, the Netherlands, and Italy*. Bournemouth: EnDOW. Available at: http://diligentsearch.eu/wp-content/uploads/2016/05/EnDOW_Report-1.pdf (accessed on 11 October 2017).

Fishman, Stephen (2017) *The Public Domain. How to Find and Use Copyright-Free Writings, Music, Art and More*. 8th ed., Berkeley: NOLO.

Fossati, Giovanna (2009) *From Grain to Pixel: The Archival Life of Film in Transition*. Amsterdam: Amsterdam University Press.

Gorini, Sabina (2004) 'The Protection of Cinematographic Heritage in Europe'. *IRIS Plus, a supplement to IRIS, Legal Observations of the European Audiovisual Observatory*, 08, pp. 1–8.

Gowers, Andrew (2006) *Gowers Review of Intellectual Property*. HM Treasury.

Hargreaves, Ian (2011) *The Hargreaves Review of Intellectual Property and Growth*. Independent report [Online]. Available at: http://www.ipo.gov.uk/ipreview-final-report.pdf (accessed on 21 April 2016).

Hediger, Vinzenz (2005) 'The Original is Always Lost', in Marijke de Valck and Malte Hagener (eds.) *Cinephilia. Movies, Love and Memory*. Amsterdam: Amsterdam University Press.

Heller, Franziska, and Barbara Flueckiger (2017) Digitale Langzeitsicherung: Nachhaltige Verfügbarkeit und Verwertbarkeit von (digitalen) Filmen – Praxen, Erfahrungen, Probleme. Deliverable in the DIASTOR research project. Available at: https://diastor.ch/digitale-langzeitsicherung/ (accessed on 9 October 2017).

High Level Expert Group (HLG; i2010: Digital Libraries) (2008) *Report on Digital Preservation, Orphan Works, and Out-of-Print Works*. [Online]. Available at: http://ec.europa.eu/information_society/activities/digital_libraries/doc/hleg/reports/copyright/copyright_subgroup_final_report_26508-clean171.pdf (accessed on 21 April 2016).

Horak, Jan-Christopher (2007) 'The Gap Between 1 and 0: Digital Video and the Omissions of Film History', *Spectator*, 27(1), pp. 29–41.

Hunter, Dan (2017) 'Blockchains, Orphan Works and the Public Domain', *New Approaches to the Orphan Works Problem* [conference], Bournemouth University, 23 June.

Hugenholtz, Bernt, Antoon Quaedvlieg, and Dirk Visser (eds.) (2012) *A Century of Dutch Copyright Law: Auteurswet 1912–2012*. Amsterdam: deLex.

Lessig, Lawrence (2001) *The Future of Ideas: The Fate of the Commons in a Connected World*. New York: Random House.

Lessig, Lawrence (2004) *Free Culture: How Big Media Uses Technology and the Law to Lock Down Culture and Control Creativity*. New York: The Penguin Press.

Lessig, Lawrence (2008) *Remix: Making Art and Commerce Thrive in the Hybrid Economy*. New York: The Penguin Press.

Lessig, Lawrence (2008) 'Little Orphan Artworks' [Op-Ed] *New York Times*, 20 May 2008.

Mazzanti, Nicola (ed.) (2011) *Digital Agenda for the European Film Heritage; Challenges of the Digital Era for Film Heritage Institutions*, Final Report prepared for the European Commission, DG Information Society and Media.

Melville, Annette, and Scott Simmon (1993) *Report of the Librarian of Congress. Film Preservation 1993. A Study of the Current State of American Film Preservation*. Washington, DC: Library of Congress [Online]. Available at: http://www.loc.gov/film/study.html (accessed on 21 April 2016).

Mendis, Dinusha (2016) 'Orphan Works', *copyrightuser*, available at: http://www.copyrightuser.org/understand/exceptions/orphan-works/ (accessed on 11 October 2017)

NFPF (ed.) (2004) *The Film Preservation Guide*. San Francisco: NFPF.

Netanel, Neil Weinstock (2008) *Copyright's Paradox*. New York: Oxford University Press.

Pallante, Maria (2012b) 'Orphan Works and Mass Digitization', *Federal Register*, 77(204), Washington, DC: Library of Congress, Copyright Office, pp. 64555–64561.

Streible, Dan (2009) 'The State of Orphan Films: Editor's Introduction', *The Moving Image, Special Issue on Orphan Film*, 9(1), pp. vi-xix.

United States Copyright Office (USCO) (2006) *Report on Orphan Works*. Washington: Library of Congress.

van Gompel, Stef (2007a) 'Audiovisual Archives and the Inability to Clear Rights in Orphan Works', *IRIS Plus, a supplement to IRIS, Legal Observations of the European Audiovisual Observatory*, 04, pp. 1–8.

van Gompel, Stef (2007b) 'Unlocking the Potential of Pre-Existing Content: How to Address the Issue of Orphan Works in Europe?', *IIC*, 6/2007, pp. 669-702.

van Gompel, Stef (2011) *Formalities in Copyright Law. An Analysis of Their History, Rationales and Possible Future*. PhD thesis, University of Amsterdam.

van Gompel, Stef, and Bernt Hugenholtz (2010) 'The Orphan Works Problem: The Copyright Conundrum of Digitizing Large-Scale Audiovisual Archives, and How to Solve It', *Popular Communication. The International Journal of Media and Culture*, 8(1), pp. 61–71.

ABOUT THE AUTHOR

Claudy Op den Kamp is Lecturer in Film and faculty member at the Centre for Intellectual Property Policy and Management at Bournemouth University, UK, and Adjunct Research Fellow at Swinburne Law School, Australia.

CHAPTER 4

A Vehicle of Power

Recategorization III – The public domain film (or, what orphan films are not)

Op den Kamp, Claudy, *The Greatest Films Never Seen. The Film Archive and the Copyright Smokescreen.* Amsterdam University Press, 2018

DOI: 10.5117/9789462981393_CH04

ABSTRACT

This chapter considers public domain films. Although public domain works should not pose any legal restrictions, they are not necessarily publicly accessible. An example from EYE's collection demonstrates how archival access is not only controlled by the rights owners but also by those who (exclusively) own the material assets.

KEYWORDS
BEYOND THE ROCKS, public domain, digital skew, public access

BEYOND THE ROCKS (US 1922, Dir. Sam Wood)
(courtesy of EYE Film Institute)

This chapter considers quadrants 3 and 4 of the legal cross section: public domain films. These fall into two quadrants because, although they belong to a category of works that should not pose any legal restrictions, they are not necessarily publicly accessible. An example from EYE's collection demonstrates how archival access is not only controlled by the rights owners but also by those who (exclusively) own the material assets. Other international examples show that some films are part of a so-called 'theoretical public domain', as they are not practically available, while others appear to be hyper-visible simply because, in certain circumstances, they are the 'easiest' to reuse.

The film archive is a site of 'knowledge production' (which, as Foucault (1972) argues, is realized through a set of specific relations), and is subject to copyright law. However, it also resists these constraints: it makes productive use of copyright by controlling the dissemination of its holdings. The chapter looks at some of these productive practices of resistance, including the way in which the archive provides access to its public domain works, actively shaping their potential to contribute to the film-historical record. The focus on access to orphan films in the previous chapter and to public domain films in this one helps illuminate how the archival institution, through the control of its filmic products, has become a contingent element of film history. The archive is therefore a 'vehicle of power' – an active site of agency and resistance.

CLOSE-UP: *BEYOND THE ROCKS*

Film collectors are often eccentric figures, and Dutch film collector Joop van Liempd was no exception. He collected just about everything – from feature films, documentaries, and television films, to rushes and outtakes – but he had a special fondness for films of the silent period (shot on inflammable nitrate stock). He owned seven warehouses in the Dutch city of Haarlem, just outside Amsterdam, to store his collection. As befitting the image of an eccentric collector, van Liempd was also somewhat paranoid: when a film had seven reels, for example, he would (for 'safety reasons') put each reel in a different warehouse.[1] This practice meant that, although his collection potentially held invaluable gems, it was impenetrable (VPRO, 2004). The Nederlands Filmmuseum was aware of the rumours that van Liempd held numerous lost films from the silent era, and, when he died in 2000, it was quick to acquire his collection – all 2,000 film cans – transferring the films to its nitrate vaults.

Cataloguing the entire collection was a slow process. Most of the cans had not been opened for a long time, and some of the material was in a state of advanced decomposition. So, from time to time, the collections department at the museum organized a 'nitrate day'. In case of a possible buildup of toxic fumes inside the cans, these days were held only when the weather was clear and dry, so that the task could be executed outside. Obviously, the Dutch weather did not allow for many 'nitrate days'. An entire team of staff, interns, and volunteers would descend upon the archive, and, as there were no contents lists, they would open the mostly unlabelled cans one by one. In the first round of identification, they noted down any obvious or visible details, including the film format, whether the film was a positive or a negative, and any colour schemes. Intertitles were also inspected for useful information, including production company logos and names, as well as language.

Early in this identification process, one of the curators came across an intertitle that bore the name of a character: 'Theodora Fitzgerald'. Most of the films had Dutch intertitles, and names were often changed in translation, but the curator noted it down anyway. It turned out that the name had not been translated, and a quick Google search pointed to an incredible find (VPRO, 2004). The name on the intertitle could mean that they had found BEYOND THE ROCKS, a lost film from 1922, directed by Sam Wood – and the only film in which the two megastars of silent cinema, Gloria Swanson and Rudolph Valentino, starred together. The film was highly sought-after on an international scale, if only for its rarity value: stars of such calibre were hardly ever paired on-screen, and this film was the first of its kind. Up to that moment, it had been assumed that all that survived of BEYOND THE ROCKS was a photographic record.

It took the Nederlands Filmmuseum the larger part of three years to discover all seven reels of the film (Fossati, 2009). Often, the museum despaired that it would find all the missing cans amongst the scrambled-up collection – but it did. In late 2003, the story came full circle: the first reel, which announced the title and the stars, was the very last reel to be found (VPRO, 2004). The film's discovery, 80 years after it was made, made news around the world, but for the world to see it, the film had first to be restored.

BEYOND THE ROCKS was originally produced and distributed by Paramount Pictures in the US, with a theatrical release date of 1922. As its US publishing date fell before 1923, the film was in the public domain.[2] This makes BEYOND THE ROCKS an ideal case study of the relationship between a film's legal status and its digital distribution. We saw earlier that the distinction between intellectual and material property is particularly interesting when the film is held by a public-sector institution. However, this film holds even greater interest as it allows us to explore what happens when the rights to a work have expired and the safeguarding institution has exclusive control of the unique physical material. Arguably, it was only due to this particular combination – the material's public domain status plus the fact that the only known material resurfaced in a public-sector institution – that it was restored and re-released at all.

BEYOND THE ROCKS was produced and distributed in 1922 and was initially in copyright for 28 years. Although the rediscovery of the film was a worldwide sensation, its initial release was not that successful. The teaming of the two stars caused huge excitement, but the reviewers were not very kind, and, over time, the film dropped off the radar. When the time came, Paramount did not renew the copyright to the film, although the reason why is unknown. The major Hollywood studios generally took care to renew their films; however, occasionally, they did make mistakes.

What we do know is that, around 1950, Paramount's focus had moved on from silent films. They were no longer in vogue; sound had taken over. The studio was now making hugely successful films, such as SUNSET BOULEVARD – also starring Gloria Swanson. BEYOND THE ROCKS was missing from the 1966 Swanson retrospective at the George Eastman House, despite the archive's efforts to ensure that the programme was exhaustive (Welsch, 2013). In 1980, the film star mentioned in her autobiography, *Swanson on Swanson*, that she had been and was still looking for a copy of the film. So, not only was the film out of copyright, it also seemed as if Paramount no longer held any of the film's materials.

The Nederlands Filmmuseum did not need permission from Paramount to restore BEYOND THE ROCKS because the film, and the novel by Elinor Glyn that it was based on, were already in the public domain. It became one of the first entirely digitally restored feature films in the world and a showpiece for both the Nederlands Filmmuseum and Haghefilm Conservation, the Dutch laboratory that carried out the restoration. The restoration itself, in 2004, was a huge project for all the partners involved, in terms of investment, technologies, and exposure. Combining analogue and digital tools, the museum restored a total of seven different versions of the film, including Dutch, English, as well as silent and sound versions, with the addition of a newly composed musical score (Fossati, 2009). It was not difficult to prove the film's historic worth and secure external funding for its ambitious digital restoration – ING Real Estate paid the bill, an estimated 200,000 euros. Paramount, as the original producer and distributor, did *not* help to restore or re-release 'its' film.

In the course of the restoration, the film's correct editing was reconstructed and the Dutch intertitles were replaced with English ones. This was accomplished with the help of the continuity script held in the Paramount Scripts Collection at the Margaret Herrick Library in Los Angeles (Fossati, 2009). Although it was also in the public domain, the Nederlands Filmmuseum, out of courtesy, asked for Paramount's permission to use the script as the basis for the new intertitles. After all, the studio co-controlled the access to the material holding of the public domain script.

Representatives of Paramount have never officially commented on their noninvolvement in the film's restoration and release. However, in 2010, Barry Allen, former executive director of film preservation at Paramount, agreed to an interview with the author. Although he did not wish to comment on the specific case, he did address the studio's general approach to film preservation:

> Motion picture preservation depends on a solid copyright [...]. The costs are enormous and copyright gives the incentive and the ability to recoup that kind of cost. [...] Sometimes a film gets lost because the rights change hands and it goes into storage or it gets moved [...]. [I]t goes into somebody's estate; you lose trails [...]. But I can't think of anything [in the Paramount library] that's really important that might have slipped through. [...] If there were copyright renewals still in place, I think they would be much more likely not to miss a renewal now, because I don't know of anybody who doesn't think there is something out there that hasn't any value at all, no matter how bad it is. You're probably going to be able to use it. (Allen, 2010)

But BEYOND THE ROCKS did 'slip through'. Allen's comments therefore lead to the tentative conclusion that the film was not that important to the studio. Had the film still been in copyright, it might not have been 'lost'. However, that does not mean that the film would have been publicly accessible: the studio might have decided not to distribute it at all if it calculated that any potential income would not cover the investment needed for its restoration. With only a couple of thousand DVD copies, it could have easily been too small a release for Paramount to bother with. Also, as the film was in the public domain, there was no protection against possible infringement.

The restored film had both a theatrical release and a DVD release that was licensed to Milestone Film, a US independent film distribution company. EYE claims the theatrical as well as the DVD and television distribution rights of the film for the Benelux countries (Belgium, Netherlands, Luxembourg) and licensed distributor Milestone for all other countries (Milestone Film & Video, 2005). The archival community often debates the issue of whether certain kinds of restorations could be seen as original versions worthy of protection in their own right (Koerber, 2008; Klimpel, 2011). The Nederlands Filmmuseum claimed copyright for the restored version of BEYOND THE ROCKS, as the closing credits show, and Milestone filed a copy of the film at the Library of Congress Copyright Office in the name of the Nederlands Filmmuseum – this is often done when changes are made to a public domain film (Fishman, 2017). The creative interventions in the restoration, such as a new tinting scheme and added score, could be considered minimally creative and therefore open to a copyright claim (of course, they would not cause the 're-copyrighting' of the original public domain film). Registering the film with the Copyright Office, however, does not necessarily mean that the claim would hold up in court. So far, however, there is an absence of case law on these issues.

WHAT IS THE PUBLIC DOMAIN?

The public domain is often defined in terms of what it is *not* – that is, the opposite of copyright, or the 'gummy residue left behind when all the good stuff has been covered by property law' (Boyle, 2008, p. 40). In *Rethinking Copyright: History, Language, Theory*, Ronan Deazley (2006) establishes the concept of the public domain, using several steps to arrive at a legal cross section of the intellectual commons. More specifically, he systematically explores the terminology to gradually reveal some of the complexities associated with the concept, such as the notion of 'exclusive control over the physical object' (p. 123). This notion proves an essential part of the definition when it comes to examining access in film archives: although public domain works can be used without permission, this does not mean that they are publicly accessible. Archives are therefore involved in what Deazley goes on to describe as the 'significant opportunity for interplay between the ownership of the physical object, [...] and the ability to control the subsequent use and dissemination of the work' (p. 124). Intellectual access implies material access: availability and public accessibility are not only controlled by those who own the rights, but also by those who own the physical assets – this is perhaps especially the case after the rights have expired – with far-reaching consequences for the visibility of the films.

Public domain works are important as a repository of raw material. This is particularly the case for cultural heritage institutions. As James Boyle (2008, pp. 39-41) argues, the public domain is the 'basis for our art, our science, and our self-understanding. It is the raw material from which we make new inventions and create new cultural works'. And he goes on to say: 'The public domain is the place we quarry the building blocks of our culture. It is, in fact, the majority of our culture' (Boyle, 2008, p. 64) Not only can public domain materials be used as an intellectual foundation, but they can also be reused materially – for example, by artists who work with extant material. According to Boyle (2003), the real difficulty lies not in validating the public domain's relevance (his position is that the public domain is the actual goal of copyright rather than its 'residue'), but in defining its exact scope. This difficulty inhibits certain uses of material in the public domain.

The challenge of defining the public domain has two aspects. First, it is difficult to determine exactly which films are part of the public domain. Leaving aside certain exceptions to the reuse of a work, Boyle (2003, p. 62) argues '[t]here is not one public domain, but many', with no true consensus as to what is in and what is out of the public domain. Secondly, a work can still be within the period of copyright in one country but in the public domain in another, according to the different national rules applicable to protection or duration (Dusollier, 2010). In an article in which she tries to map this 'uncharted terrain', Pamela Samuelson (2003, p. 148) summarizes the public domain as 'different sizes at different times and in different countries'. Deazley (2006, p. 130) adds that the 'public domain [...] is a historically, geographically, culturally, socially and politically contingent concept, as are all intellectual properties'. Within the context of the film archive, this variability can greatly complicate the task of distributing such works online. Online distribution entails making the works available in many countries simultaneously, so it is important to be able to determine what part of the collection is solidly in the public domain (everywhere).

There are several ways in which works can become public domain. Copyright 'comes into existence from the point of creation' (Deazley, 2006, p. 102), and one of the most straightforward ways in which a work enters the public domain is when that copyright expires. In the US, for instance, the copyright of a work might also have been forfeited because of a failure to comply with the technical formalities in effect at the time, or a work might be categorically excluded from copyright protection, as some governmental works are (Donaldson, 2014). What is important to note in the context of the argument this book puts forward is that, what is left in the archives, after works have entered the public domain and are no longer owned intellectually, is the material property, and there is room for exploiting that material property.

Aside from the different shapes the public domain can take based on what is believed to fall within or outside its sphere, there is also a distinction between what could be considered a *practical* versus a *theoretical* public domain. A theoretical public domain comprises works that are in the public domain in theory but, as Samuelson (2003, p. 149) demonstrates, do not really 'reside there' in practice: 'A painting from the mid-nineteenth century that remains in a private collection or was destroyed in a fire is, in theory, in the public domain as a matter of copyright law, but its non-public nature or its destruction mean that it may, in fact, be there only in theory.' Theoretically, public domain works can be appropriated and used by anyone without the need to seek the permission of a rights holder, but exclusive ownership of the physical materials and control of their dissemination can adversely affect this situation – they can become *less* accessible. This chapter argues that, just like a mid-nineteenth century painting in a private collection, some of the public domain works held by film archives only reside in a theoretical public domain; they do not reside in a practical public domain due to the combination of their nonpublic nature and the archive's exclusive ownership of the physical materials.[3]

Some of the literature calling for a larger public domain expresses concern over the lack of availability of some of the public domain works that lie hidden in the archive behind various administrative layers (Lange, 1982; Litman, 1990; Samuelson, 2003; Lessig, 2004; 2006; 2008; Boyle, 2008), but only more recent studies have started to take into consideration the repercussions of this situation for the study of the materials (Wallace, 2016; Deazley, 2017).

The focus on access to public domain films reveals that the nature of the archive plays a role in shaping access. Different kinds of archives provide access to their public domain materials in very different ways. Commercial archives, on the one hand, often own the copyright to most of their holdings and frequently prefer to exploit these materials rather than their public domain holdings. The next section of this chapter looks at an example of a studio archive in more detail. Public-sector archives, on the other hand, own or hold on deposit the material property but seldom the rights to the films they safeguard (Thompson, 2007), so, for distribution purposes, they benefit if the rights to their works have expired. The chapter also looks at several examples of this practice.

The digital skew

In an article discussing the detrimental consequences of copyright challenges impeding the clearance of moving image material for digital use, Sally McCausland, senior lawyer at Australian broadcaster SBS, addresses what she terms the 'digital' or 'blockbuster skew':

> The sense of history which comes with access to the whole, or a substantial part, of an archive, is of much greater cultural value than a small selection curated through the random prism of copyright clearance. [...]
> There is a danger that in the digital age the publicly available cultural history [...] will skew: we will remain familiar with ubiquitous blockbuster

programs which are available [...] more than we will remember local [...] programs left in the archives. (McCausland, 2009, p. 160)

The digital skew – the asymmetry between analogue and digitized collections – is primarily attributed to the gridlock of copyright, which stretches from its role in the selection of material for digitization to its block on making material publicly available (Hudson and Kenyon, 2007). Indeed, some categories of works are considered too legally 'difficult' and are not prioritized for digitization and public viewing. As the previous chapter argues, orphan works pose particular problems for those archives involved in large-scale digitization projects. It seems, however, that less obvious categories of works also contribute to this digital skew. If even a legally unrestricted category, such as that of public domain works, plays a role in this outcome, then positing the digital skew as an exclusively legal paradigm risks neglecting other, archival factors. This is the main reason why this study considers public domain films separately from orphan films, despite the fact that both categories have, for the most part, lost their financial incentive for further preservation and sometimes have a similar impact on archival and studio practice. By examining access to public domain material, this chapter aims to shift the debate away from exclusively legal territory.

The public domain and public access

In an article analyzing digitization practices in Australian cultural institutions, Emily Hudson and Andrew Kenyon (2007, pp. 199-200) conclude that '[c]opyright has had a significant impact on digitisation practices to date, including in the selection of material to digitise and the circumstances in which it is made publicly available [...] and has driven the content of online exhibitions, galleries and databases'. It is safe to say that this conclusion applies to more countries than just Australia, and that copyright defines online content in both for-profit and not-for-profit contexts.

The differences in practice between the different kinds of archives are particularly visible in the shift from analogue to digital distribution as reproduction becomes (relatively) easier. The US DVD-on-demand initiative, Warner Archive Online, exemplifies the for-profit environment in which public domain works are rapidly fading from public view: in this archive, *no* public domain titles are made available. The most glaring absence is that of pre-1923 films, but public domain titles from later years are also missing. In contrast, Celluloid Remix, an online remix contest using early Dutch films, is an example of an initiative by public-sector archives in which public domain works are hyper-visible. The contest, which took place for the first time in 2009, consists of exclusively public domain material. Below, we look at some of these examples in more detail.

EXAMPLES OF PUBLIC DOMAIN FILMS FADING FROM PUBLIC VIEW

1. Warner Archive Online

A studio archive will own the copyright to most of its holdings and can therefore make an upfront investment in the preservation and subsequent dissemination of the work with relative ease. It is simpler for the studio to recoup some of the costs if a work is in copyright, not least because any potential infringement of a distributed title can be controlled. Some of the studio's archival holdings, however, will be in the public domain – for example, if the rights to the film have expired or been forfeited because of legal technicalities.[4] The studio's inability to control potential infringement problems in the case of distributed public domain titles significantly lessens the attraction of pursuing their digital or online dissemination.

Given this, it is not surprising that a studio such as Warner Bros. chooses to reduce and heavily police public accessibility to its (digitized) public domain works. Warner's George Feltenstein, speaking at the 'Reimagining the Archive' conference at UCLA in November 2010, inadvertently drew attention to this policy.[5] Presenting the studio's new DVD-on-demand website,[6] he stated that of around 7,800 Warner feature films,[7] some 4,100 were once distributed on VHS, and, in 2009, some 1,700 features had come out on DVD. The DVD-on-demand website was launched in March 2009, starting with 150 digitized titles; two years later, it had reached approximately 1,000, including '10% of the library that likely would not have made it to DVD before' (Feltenstein, 2010). Warner appears to be tapping into an apparently new niche for archival material, as these 1,000 titles were not exclusively theatrical feature films that had been on release; they also included previously undistributed short subject collections.

At the same time, however, although Feltenstein (2010) declared that the ultimate goal was to 'make the whole Warner library available to everyone with the best possible quality', the site appears to feature hardly any public domain titles – and very possibly none. This is most perceptible in the absence of films with a pre-1923 theatrical release date,[8] the US cutoff date before which all creative works are deemed to be automatically public domain. However, more research would be needed to establish more precisely how many surviving titles currently owned by Warner Bros. were released pre-1923, as well as how many later titles in its collection are actually in the public domain. (At the time of writing, the site has been transformed into a streaming service, and the earliest films featured are from 1928 and 1929.)

2. The Criterion Collection

The Criterion Collection's DVD distribution provides another example of a company that understandably favours titles that are clearly in copyright over those in the public domain. An immediate and important distinction from Warner Bros., however, is that Criterion does not own a film collection as such, but distributes films on DVD[9] after acquiring the licensing rights from an external party. In his role as advisor and consulting producer at Criterion, Robert Fischer has affirmed that the label would never distribute public domain titles.[10] Of the various selection criteria the company considers, the very first is a 'secure rights situation'; only once this is established will it look at whether the particular title fits within the rest of the collection.[11] Licensing content from third-party rights holders brings its own problems: over the years, it has become increasingly hard to obtain (continuing) licensing rights to produce DVDs of popular studio films. 'One unfortunate result of this situation is that many of the excellent supplements [that were] available on the company's laserdiscs languish without an outlet' (Parker and Parker, 2011, p. 184).

These are but two examples of large-scale digital-access projects that seem to pay little or no attention to public domain titles. Clear copyright ownership and licensing agreements are necessary if a company wishes to produce an attractive product whose sale will guarantee that some of the remastering and restoration costs will be recouped. It seems safe to say that, in the shift from analogue to digital distribution, far fewer public domain titles are made available in the for-profit environment; in fact, they are fading from public view.[12] 'Not only does this undermine the rationale of copyright expiration and the public domain, but it harms the public domain by restricting access to works intended to be used for cultural reproduction' (Wallace, 2015). The business models of commercial studios, however, clearly stand in stark contrast to the mandates and practices of institutions in the not-for-profit environment.

EXAMPLES OF PUBLIC DOMAIN FILMS BECOMING HYPER-VISIBLE

As public archives seldom own the rights to the films they own or hold on deposit, they benefit if the rights to these works have expired. However, just as in a for-profit environment, these archives have to make choices about what material to make accessible. The high costs of the restoration, digitization, and continued preservation of film material mean that, even if an archive has a mandate that requires it to ensure its material is publicly available, it still has to make selections. For this reason, public-sector archives are also involved in what Deazley (2006, p. 124), as mentioned above, calls the 'interplay between the ownership of the physical object [...] and the ability to control the subsequent use and dissemination'. The following two examples show how the public archive specifically foregrounds public domain material.

1. The Internet Archive

Some online initiatives are made up exclusively, or at least in large part, of public domain material. One example is the Internet Archive, a not-for-profit initiative established in the mid-1990s in San Francisco.[13] Aside from open access to public domain books, the site also provides online access to historical audiovisual collections via collaborations with external partners, such as the Library of Congress. However, it contains 'only public-domain items, including the ever-popular DUCK AND COVER [a 1951 American civil defence film aimed at children], allowing it [...] to avoid the problem of copyright. Similarly, the Library of Congress gives access primarily to [out of copyright] films in the pre-1915 era' (Thompson, 2007).

2. 'Images for the Future' projects

Other initiatives include projects that have been developed as part of the Dutch national digitization project 'Images for the Future' – for example, the video-on-demand platform, Ximon, and online remix contest, Celluloid Remix.[14] One of Ximon's remits was to avoid the uploaded material's legal status dominating the character of the portal. However, the most important factor determining what was presented online was, as former EYE curator Emjay Rechsteiner (2010) made clear, 'what was clearable', and therefore included a large proportion of public domain works. Various other factors, such as the physical condition of the material or how much restoration a film would need, were subsequently taken into consideration.[15] Meanwhile, Celluloid Remix (mentioned earlier), an online remix contest featuring early Dutch films, was exclusively made up of public domain material.

The consequences for the material's potential for 'history making' are evident when it comes to considering access to works in the public domain. In a commercial context, the films' public domain status, in combination with the exclusive ownership of the source materials, renders them invisible. As a business model this is completely understandable: a for-profit archive does not have any interest in distributing its public domain titles as it makes no financial sense to invest capital in an asset that cannot be protected. 'For a studio, funds are better spent on owned, but unexploited assets in need of restoration – with no rights intangibles' (*A Matter of Rights*, 2010). In a not-for-profit context, however, that same combination of factors facilitates easier digital distribution, and can even lead to what the curator of the Danish Film Institute, Thomas Christensen, in a presentation at the 2010 'Archiving the Future' conference in York (UK), has labelled a 'freak show': a unilateral representation of audiovisual public domain materials on various online platforms, or a *hyper-visibility* of certain titles.

The public domain and access to high-quality originals

As the examples above show, the potential conflation of rights in property and rights in intellectual property is most apparent in public domain works, and, as a consequence, archival policy can lead to either underexposure or over-exposure of such films. The fact that a work is in the public domain does not necessarily mean that it is freely available for use:

> Even though a work is in the public domain, the physical substance in which it is embodied [...] is usually still owned by somebody. [...] [T]he owner enjoys all the rights of any personal property owner. This means the owner may restrict or even deny public access to the work or charge for access or the right to make copies. This is usually not a problem for written works, which can be found in bookstores, libraries, and archives, but it is a problem for other types of works. (Fishman, 2017, p. 11)

Valuable works of art are one example.[16] Film, of course, is another. The Warner Online Archive is a for-profit example of the fact that lack of protection 'cannot in itself impose free access to the copies of public domain works' (Dusollier, 2010, p. 8). The case of BEYOND THE ROCKS, on the other hand, provides a nonprofit example in which no other copy of the work was available except the unique material preserved by the archive.

The right to grant or restrict access is nothing new; as a property right, it was very much part of the analogue era. However, in the digital era, material can be reused relatively easily by almost anyone, on a potentially (online) global scale. Digitization has changed the way that access to works in the public domain is controlled. In visual art and film, for instance, there are many examples in which various degraded copies of a work float about (online) while one entity can and does restrict access to the highest quality 'original'.

In film, it is common practice not to allow the public access to the highest-quality original, as this material tends to remain in the safekeeping of the archive, with a view to making subsequent reproductions. Films exist by the grace of reproduction, and the 'experience' of the film – in projection - is often enjoyed quite separately from the physical object, with the concept of the 'original' being a contested notion. In the case of a painting, for instance, it is quite the reverse: it is generally thought that the 'real' experience is guaranteed only by seeing the unique, original work.

In light of these different kinds of experiences in which we often deal with (degraded) copies, we need to bear in mind the diversity of the different kinds of reproductions, and the ways in which these reproductions are 'transhistorical messengers of values' (Codell, 2010, p. 219): they mark what was possible in a given period, and how that differs from what is possible in other periods.

Let us consider the case of Stanley Donen's 1963 film, CHARADE, which not only exposes the rigour with which copyright law is applied, but also illustrates that proven historic worth is often a determining factor in the provision of access to public domain works of the highest possible quality. Originally produced and distributed by Universal Pictures, the film became public domain as soon as it was released because it had not met the strict compliance requirements in place in the US. A pre-1978 film could only be published in the US with a proper copyright notice.[17] This consisted of three elements: 1) the word *copyright* or the © symbol; 2) the name of the copyright owner; and 3) the date of first publication. If it omitted any of these, then, under the copyright law in force for films created before 1 January 1978, the work would enter the public domain the moment of its publication (Fishman, 2017).

The relevant frames of the opening credits of CHARADE read: 'MCMLXIII BY UNIVERSAL PICTURES COMPANY, INC and STANLEY DONEN FILMS, INC ALL RIGHTS RESERVED'. In an article addressing why several classic films from the studio era became public domain, David Pierce (2007, p. 130) explains: 'It is obvious today, but no one noticed at the time that this notice is missing the word *copyright* or the ©.' As a consequence, CHARADE fell into the public domain at the moment of its publication.

The most essential element for further distribution of a work is access to a material copy, especially when it is in the public domain and can be copied and distributed without the need for prior permission from the copyright owner. It is unclear when exactly the realization hit that the notice was faulty, but the film was widely distributed and many parties had material access to film copies of CHARADE. This has led to the production of many different editions, both on VHS and DVD. Over the decades, the film has proven to be wildly successful with audiences; obviously, its popularity may have been helped by its heightened visibility due to its status as a public domain film.

When a film was first published in the US with no copyright notice within a certain time period, it entered the public domain. However, this only applies to the US; the film does not automatically become public domain in any other country. When calculating how long the copyright in a foreign work lasts, many countries use 'the rule of the shorter term'. It provides that 'unless the legislation of that country otherwise provides, the term of protection shall not exceed the term fixed in the country of origin of the work' (Kamina, 2016, p. 483). In the Netherlands, which observes this rule of the shorter term, CHARADE is considered to be in the public domain. Switzerland, however, does not adhere to this rule, and defines the authors of a film as the director, the cinematographer, and the composer of the music – but not the entity that produced it. Copyright duration is based on the life of these authors, plus 70 years after the death of the last to survive. At the time of writing, Stanley Donen is alive, so CHARADE is still in copyright in Switzerland, and will be for at least another 70 years (see also note 55).

The film has been in circulation for many years in various 'unofficial' versions of differing quality. In 2004, Universal, which had sole access to the highest quality original negatives, decided to license 'the only authorized professional transfer' exclusively to Criterion (Dessem, 2006): aware of the undiminished public appetite for the film, the studio opted to go for quality. Although the specific layout of the DVD (including added value) is protected, the main feature itself remains public domain in many countries.[18] This scenario, however, should probably be seen as an exception as the film's historic worth was already proven.[19]

The last three chapters have addressed the quadrants of the legal cross section presented in Chapter 1, focusing on digital access to embargoed films, orphan films, and films in the public domain. The next chapter explores these access activities as a whole, converging in found-footage filmmaking, and looks at the role that the institutional context plays in this intervention, in which archival films (the raw ingredients) are transformed into new products.

NOTES

1   The information in this close-up is mainly derived from two programmes that are available on the Milestone DVD release of BEYOND THE ROCKS: one is a documentary by Dutch broadcaster VPRO made for its TV programme RAM (April 2004) about the discovery of the film; the other is a short piece, entitled 'The Restoration of BEYOND THE ROCKS', produced by EYE and narrated by Giovanna Fossati, who was responsible for its restoration.

2   Indeed, in the US, any work with an authorized publication date from before 1923 is automatically in the public domain. However, a work 'created or first published in the United States that is now in the public domain in the United States will also be in the public domain in all countries that follow the rule of the shorter term. This will be the case even though the work would not be in the public domain under the foreign country's own copyright law. For example, all works first published in the United States before 1923 are in the public domain in the United States and are, therefore, in the public domain in all the countries that follow the rule of the shorter term. Without the rule, many of these works would not be in the public domain in these foreign countries, based on their own copyright laws' (Fischman, 2017, pp. 298-299). The Netherlands follows the rule of the shorter

term, and, as an extension, EYE, for all practical purposes, considers works that are in the public domain in the US because of nonrenewal or faulty notices also to be in the public domain in the Netherlands. This is done based on article 42 of the Dutch Copyright Act, which states 'Notwithstanding the provisions of this chapter, no copyright can be invoked in the Netherlands in cases where the duration has already expired in the country of origin of the work. What is stipulated in the first sentence does not apply to works whose maker is a national of a Member State of the European Union or of a State party to the Agreement on the European Economic Area of 2 May 1992.'

3   An additional factor inhibiting a film's visibility, predominantly seen in the US, is the issue of personality rights. Films can be in the public domain, but their access can be restricted by individuals depicted in the films if proper clearances were not received. Ambitious and litigious heirs often feature large in these scenarios.

4   David Pierce (2007) provides numerous examples of classic studio films.

5   At the time, Feltenstein was senior vice president of theatrical catalogue marketing at Warner Archive Collection Online.

6   What started as www.warnerarchive.com was redirected in April 2016 to www. wbshop.com, where other Warner Bros. products were sold, such as clothing and toys. In 2010, Feltenstein commented: 'The DVDs are created on demand, professionally authored, and ship within two or three days' (to the US only). At the time of writing, the site had turned into a streaming service (accessed on 14 October 2017).

7   These titles are not exclusively Warner-produced feature films: several mergers and takeovers have led to what is currently a quite eclectic film collection, including several other film libraries, such as the pre-1986 MGM library.

8   As Warner Bros. was officially incorporated in 1923, pre-1923 films would include such titles as those produced by First National Films, which later merged with Warner Bros. (Finler, 2003). Titles that used to be sold on the same website from both the MGM Limited Editions and Sony Pictures Choice Collection in 2016 also did not include any pre-1930 titles (accessed on 12 April 2016).

9   This is also called the 'film school in a box' (Parker and Parker, 2011, p. 70).

10 He did so in a presentation to the 2010 Gorizia International Film Studies Spring School.

11 An obvious exception to the policy seems to be NANOOK OF THE NORTH (US 1922, Robert Flaherty), which was released on DVD by Criterion in 1999 (as #33). The title is a US film with a release date before 1923, the defining reason for a film to become a public domain title.

12 For excellent previous research about the fading of works into the public domain, see Christopher Buccafusco and Paul Heald (2013) and Heald (2014).

13 Available at: https://archive.org/ (accessed on 15 October 2017).

14 Information on these projects is available at: http://www.beeldenvoordetoekomst. nl/en/activities/celluloid-remix.html (accessed on 12 April 2016).

15 In the absence of a further financial investor or strategic partner, Ximon halted its services in January 2014. See http://www.ximon.nl/. The rights issues in the Images for the Future mass digitization project have been vastly underestimated overall; only an extraordinarily small amount of the digitized film material is available online (approximately 2%). This information was provided by Kennisland's Paul Keller during the final EnDOW project meeting at the EUIPO in Alicante on 15 May 2018.

16 Andrea Wallace (2015, 2016) has conducted some excellent research on this topic.

17 'Distributed and shown to the general public in movie theaters' (Fishman, 2017, p. 168).

18 Individual elements of the film, such as the underlying story or theme song may well be still in copyright, but for the purposes of the film, the whole of elements is considered to be public domain.

19 Another example of a film that has proven its historic worth through its public domain status and, therefore, keeps seeing new high quality iterations, is IT'S A WONDERFUL LIFE (US 1946, Frank Capra)

BIBLIOGRAPHY

A Matter of Rights: A Talk with Lee Tsiantis (2010) Available at: http://selfstyledsiren. blogspot.ch/2010/02/matter-of-rights-talk-with-lee-tsiantis.html (accessed on 21 April 2016).

Allen, Barry ([retired] Executive Director of Broadcast Services and Film Preservation, Paramount Pictures) (2010) Interviewed by Claudy Op den Kamp. Philadelphia, US, 4 November.

Boyle, James (2003) 'The Second Enclosure Movement and the Construction of the Public Domain', *Law and Contemporary Problems*, 66, pp. 33–74.

Boyle, James (2008) *The Public Domain: Enclosing the Commons of the Mind.* New Haven: Yale University Press.

Buccafusco, Chris, and Paul Heald (2013) 'Do Bad Things Happen When Works Fall into the Public Domain? Empirical Tests of Copyright Term Extension', *Berkeley Tech. L.J.*, 28(1), pp. 1–43.

Codell, Julie (2010) '"Second Hand Images": On Art's Surrogate Means and Media-Introduction', *Visual Resources*, 26(3), pp. 214-215.

Deazley, Ronan (2006) *Rethinking Copyright: History, Theory, Language.* Northampton: Edward Elgar.

Deazley, Ronan (2017) 'Copyright 101', *Copyright Cortex* [online] available at: https:// copyrightcortex.org/copyright-101 (accessed on 25 September 2017).

Dessem, Matthew (2006) '#57: CHARADE', *The Criterion Contraption*, 2 July. [Online]. Available at: http://criterioncollection.blogspot.com/2006_07_01_archive.html (accessed on 21 April 2016).

Donaldson, Michael (2014) *Clearance & Copyright. Everything You Need to Know for Film and Television*. 4th ed. West Hollywood: Silman-James Press.

Dusollier, Séverine (2010) *Scoping Study on Copyright and Related Rights and the Public Domain*. Namur: WIPO.

Feltenstein, George (2010) 'New Platforms', *Re-imagining the Archive. Remapping and Remixing Traditional Models in the Digital Era*, University of California Los Angeles, 10-12 November 2010.

Finler, Joel (2003) *The Hollywood Story*. London and New York: Wallflower Press.

Fishman, Stephen (2017) *The Public Domain. How to Find and Use Copyright-Free Writings, Music, Art and More*. 8th ed., Berkeley: NOLO.

Fossati, Giovanna (2009) *From Grain to Pixel: The Archival Life of Film in Transition*. Amsterdam: Amsterdam University Press.

Foucault, Michel (1972) *The Archaeology of Knowledge and the Discourse on Language*. Translated by Alan Mark Sheridan-Smith. New York: Pantheon Books.

Heald, Paul (2014) 'How Copyright Keeps Works Disappeared', *Empirical Legal Studies*, 11(4), pp. 829–866.

Hudson, Emily, and Andrew Kenyon (2007) 'Digital Access: The Impact of Copyright in Digitisation Practices in Australian Museums, Galleries, Libraries and Archives', *UNSW Law Journal*, 30(1), pp. 12–52.

Kamina, Pascal (2016) *Film Copyright in the European Union*. Cambridge: Cambridge University Press.

Klimpel, Paul (ed.) (2011) *Bewegte Bilder—Starres Recht? Das Filmerbe und seine rechtlichen Rahmenbedingungen*. Berlin: Berlin Academic.

Koerber, Martin (2008) 'Why Restoration Does not Change Copyright', 64th International Federation of Film Archives (FIAF) Congress, Paris, 17-26 April.

Lange, David (1982) 'Recognizing the Public Domain', *Law and Contemporary Problems*, 44(4), pp. 147–178.

Lessig, Lawrence (2004) *Free Culture: How Big Media Uses Technology and the Law to Lock Down Culture and Control Creativity*. New York: The Penguin Press.

Lessig, Lawrence (2006) *Code: Version 2.0*. New York: Basic Books.

Lessig, Lawrence (2008) *Remix: Making Art and Commerce Thrive in the Hybrid Economy*. New York: The Penguin Press.

Litman, Jessica (1990) 'The Public Domain', *Emory Law Journal*, 39 (L.J. 965), pp. 965–1023.

McCausland, Sally (2009) 'Getting Public Broadcaster Archives Online', *Media and Arts Law Review*, 14(2), pp. 142–165.

Milestone Film & Video (2005) *BEYOND THE ROCKS* [Press release].

Parker, Mark, and Deborah Parker (2011) *The DVD and the Study of Film. The Attainable Text*. New York: Palgrave MacMillan.

Pierce, David (2007) 'Forgotten Faces: Why Some of Our Cinema Heritage Is Part of the Public Domain', *Film History*, 19, pp. 125–143.

Rechsteiner, Emjay (Curator Contemporary Dutch Film, Eye Film Institute Netherlands) (2010) Interviewed by Claudy Op den Kamp. Philadelphia, US, 6 November.

Samuelson, Pamela (2003) 'Mapping the Public Domain', *Law and Contemporary Problems*, 66(147), pp. 147–171.

Swanson, Gloria (1980) *Swanson on Swanson*. New York: Random House.

Thompson, Kristin (2007) 'The Celestial Multiplex', *Observations on Film Art* [Online]. Available at: http://www.davidbordwell.net/blog/2007/03/27/the-celestial-multiplex/ (accessed on 21 April 2016).

VPRO, 2004. RAM [television programme]. NL3. 18 April 2004.

Wallace, Andrea (2015) 'Surrogate Rights Explained', *www.surrogateiprights.org*, available at: http://surrogateiprights.org/surrogate-rights-explained/ (accessed on 14 October 2017)

Wallace, Andrea (2016) 'Cultural Institutions and Surrogate Intellectual Property Rights: Resisting an Artwork's Transfer into the Public Domain', *ISHTIP conference*, University of Glasgow, 6–8 July.

Welsch, Tricia (2013) *Gloria Swanson. Ready for her Close-Up*. Jackson: University Press of Mississippi.

ABOUT THE AUTHOR

Claudy Op den Kamp is Lecturer in Film and faculty member at the Centre for Intellectual Property Policy and Management at Bournemouth University, UK, and Adjunct Research Fellow at Swinburne Law School, Australia.

CHAPTER 5

A Birthplace
The begotten film

Op den Kamp, Claudy, *The Greatest Films Never Seen. The Film Archive* | 115
and the Copyright Smokescreen. Amsterdam University Press, 2018

DOI: 10.5117/9789462981393_CH05

ABSTRACT

This chapter explores found-footage filmmaking both within and outside of the archival context. It perceives the archive as a birthplace (or place of rebirth), where the raw material of archival films is transformed into new products. This chapter also argues that found-footage filmmaking, as a contemporary practice that advocates a 'return' to the filmic source, is by nature an act of resistance and revisionism, and foregrounds the role the archive plays in this process.

KEYWORDS
Found-footage filmmaking, aesthetics of access, (non)institutional reuse, human agency, copyright exceptions, BITS & PIECES

BITS & PIECES, NO. 367
(courtesy of EYE Film Institute)

The last three chapters considered the quadrants of the legal cross section introduced in Chapter 1, using examples of digital access practices for embargoed, orphan, and public domain films. In the process, they unravelled the implications of copyright for the film archive, and revealed how the exclusive ownership of unique source material, as well as human agency, impact public access.

This chapter looks at embargoed, orphan, and public domain films as a whole in order to explore the way found-footage filmmaking reuses these films both within and outside of the archival context. It perceives the archive as a birthplace (or place of rebirth), where the raw material of archival films is transformed into new products, and argues that found-footage filmmaking, as a contemporary practice that advocates a 'return' to the filmic source, is by nature an act of resistance and revisionism. The chapter examines how such filmmaking challenges canonical film history (and the way this history has been written) and foregrounds the role the archive plays in this process.

Found-footage filmmaking also helps highlight the crucial role of the archive as a place that safeguards legally ambiguous films that would otherwise languish in obscurity. The chapter uses EYE's BITS & PIECES collection of unidentified film fragments as a cogent example. It also explores the 'human agency' (Bandura, 2006) of the individuals working in the archive, as they decide on whether and how to activate and make available the films in their care – decisions that involve choice, restriction, and resistance. Beyond this institutional context, the (digital) work produced by found-footage filmmakers who reuse archival film with provenance that lies outside the archive has brought into focus a particular tension: their work often resists the legal constraints. This chapter looks at some examples of these practices.

FOUND FOOTAGE, LEGAL PROVENANCE, AND THE 'AESTHETICS OF ACCESS'

Found footage is footage that is 'shot for one use but then "found" and repurposed, and thus redirected toward new uses' (Anderson, 2011, p. 68): found-footage filmmaking is therefore the practice of creating new films from extant material.

This chapter turns to the legal provenance of the source material used in found-footage filmmaking, focusing on the relation of found-footage filmmaking to the concept of the 'aesthetics of access'. Lucas Hilderbrand introduced this concept in his 2009 publication, *Inherent Vice*, in which he addresses the interconnected issues of copyright, preservation, and bootlegging in the specific case of VHS. When Hilderbrand speaks of the aesthetics of access, he is referring to the formal characteristics of the image. For example, filmmaker Matthias Müller used a 16mm film camera to shoot footage from Hollywood melodramas from the 1950s and 1960s directly from a television screen in order to compile his 1990 found-footage film, HOME STORIES. He favoured this mode of production possibly for its visual effects, possibly as a method of circumventing the need to secure permission to reuse the film material, but no matter the motivation, the slightly degraded appearance of the duplicated material is a direct effect of the manner in which the material was accessed. It is in this sense that the term 'aesthetics of access' will be used in this chapter, which argues that the legal provenance of the material, as well as the techniques of circumvention used to obtain it, can be traced in the aesthetic form of found-footage films.[1] In their new, amalgamated states, these films question such concepts as ownership and authorship. Furthermore, as will become evident later in the chapter, they also emphasize the interdependent relationship between institutional context, (the activation of) copyright, and film form.

Institutional reuse

The chapter begins by focusing on so-called institutional reuse, taking EYE as a case study. EYE has long had an interest in found-footage filmmaking. The institute has invited filmmakers at the 'experimental' end of the spectrum, such as Gustav Deutsch and Bill Morrison, to work with its archive, and has acquired the found-footage films of other filmmakers – Matthias Müller, Peter Tscherkassky, Yervant Gianikian, and Angela Ricci Lucchi – for its permanent collection. EYE also used the title 'Found Footage' to announce the theme of the exhibition (and corresponding film programme) it mounted to inaugurate its new building in Amsterdam in April 2012.

The institutional context allows the archive to become a place of rebirth, where cinematic heritage becomes the raw ingredient for the genesis of new films (Leyda, 1964; Hausheer and Settele, 1992; Habib, 2006; 2007a; 2007b). In light of its sensitive relationships with donors and copyright holders, however, the archive has to respect certain intellectual property restrictions placed on the material. Nonetheless, the institutional context is also one in which archivists can intervene to enforce access to some of the collection's holdings despite legal limitations.

GUSTAV DEUTSCH AND THE FILM ARCHIVE

Austrian filmmaker Gustav Deutsch (born in Vienna in 1952) could be called a 'filmmaker without a camera', since many of his films start on the editing table. While editing, he creates a new story from extant film material, a practice he has pursued for more than 20 years. Deutsch works mainly with public archives, in contrast to other filmmakers who reuse film footage found exclusively outside the institutional context – for example, in personal film collections, flea markets, video stores, or on the internet.[2]

After completing the first installment of his 'Film Ist' series in 1998, Deutsch was invited by the Nederlands Filmmuseum to work with its material. Over the course of several weeks, the museum provided him with an editing table and unlimited access to its film collection and its preservation staff. Deutsch considers cataloguing systems as too restrictive due to their tendency to focus on search topics such as genre, title, year, name of director, or certain keywords. What he wants to find in archival film material is often very specific – for example, 'man looks through peephole' – and the collections of most film museums are not catalogued and described at this granular level. Some of the scenes Deutsch seeks can only be retrieved when someone remembers noticing their occurrence in a larger film. Consequently, he always starts by talking to archivists and other staff members. Their visual knowledge and their memory of the films in their collections mean that the archive itself becomes an active participant in the coproduction of the found-footage films rather than simply the locus of the filmmaker's research.

BITS & PIECES AND HUMAN AGENCY

Eric Thouvenel (2008, p. 99) argues that 'famous films [...] have already been authenticated, that is to say, they are *signed*. Thus, it is very difficult for found-footage filmmakers to inject meaning into the text or to say something about themselves'. Deutsch therefore uses mainly noncanonical titles and (unidentified) film fragments in order to tell his *own* story and convey his own specific vision. As mentioned earlier, EYE predominantly holds noncanonical films, and Deutsch found that its BITS & PIECES collection in particular provided a wide-ranging source for the research and production of his films.

The BITS & PIECES collection was initiated at the Nederlands Filmmuseum in the late 1980s and early 1990s by the then-deputy director, Eric de Kuyper, as a collection of short, unidentified fragments of film, which the institute preserved primarily because of the aesthetic value of their images. Although other archives collect beautiful snippets of film, EYE is the only one to have gathered them together *in order to present them*.[3]

The collection of fragments is currently central to the legal debate around orphan works. In the early 1990s, there was no such label as 'orphan works', and what is known as the 'orphan works problem' had yet to emerge. As Chapter 3 explains, orphan works are films that might still be within the period of copyright but lack an identifiable or locatable rights holder, posing a specific dilemma when it comes to the practices of digitization and public access. Some countries have a so-called preservation exception, but generally, reproducing a work and communicating it to the public are copyright-restricted activities and require the permission of the rights holder. Often, as unidentified fragments are pieces of film that lack a provenance (that is, there is no complete, identifiable copy of the work, with opening or closing credits), it cannot be determined whose permission to seek in order to use the film, or even whether it is still within the copyright period. These film fragments could be seen as orphan works *par excellence*.

Yet, copyright does not seem to be a concern restricting the reuse of the orphaned collection of BITS & PIECES: the clips have played a central role in both the collection's visibility and the sales output of the Nederlands Filmmuseum and, later, of EYE. This is remarkable in light of the particular challenges that orphan works pose for digitization and for reuse practices more generally. They have in fact been reused in numerous ways and in various projects, ranging from academic conferences to more commercial contexts – DJ Spooky has used them extensively, for example, in his 2000 show 'Les Vestiges' ('Traces') at the Louvre in Paris.[4] These practices underline a consistently neglected and under-researched component in archival access: the human agency of the institution's archivists.

As we saw earlier, the law does not consist of a set of rules that can be applied mechanically; these rules need to be activated, and someone needs to decide whether to make the material available. Archivists have the capacity to act: they can intervene and enforce access to some of the collection's holdings despite apparent legal restrictions, analyzing whether it is worth the risk of not clearing the rights for a particular reuse. Reuse could entail an infringement claim – often with monetary consequences – if a rights holder were to come forward, jeopardizing relations with (future) donors and rights holders. In the entire history of both the Nederlands Filmmuseum and EYE, however, there have been no examples of copyright infringement claims. Just as with the diligent search criteria we looked at in the previous chapter, based on the principle that highly professional archivists exercise a certain professional discretion, the risks in reusing the fragments in the BITS & PIECES collection have been judged to be very low.

Other archives, though, might come to different decisions, and, in the case of orphan works, the human agency of an institution's archivists can lead to potential creative obstacles for filmmakers. Frequently, the archive will not grant the filmmaker legal permission to reuse the works without further research into who owns the copyright. However, based on its exclusive owner-ship of the source material and its capacity to act, it can grant a filmmaker the 'material' permission for reuse. Archivists therefore tread a fine line between the ability to enforce access and what is colloquially termed, 'gatekeeping.'

The stag films Deutsch reused in his 2009 work, the last in his 'FILM IST' series, A GIRL & A GUN, exemplify this balancing act. These are brief, silent, and explicitly sexual films that were produced in the first half of the 20th century, for the most part illicitly, due to censorship laws. The films in question formed part of the film collection at the Kinsey Institute for Research in Sex, Gender and Reproduction at Indiana University. The institute initially restricted Deutsch's access to some of their holdings, 'pre-selecting' his range of possi-ble choices; it specifically declared the films on human sexual behaviour shot in the 1940s and 1950s by Alfred Kinsey himself off-limits. Remarkably, these films are not available for anyone to watch, even on the archive's premises. Deutsch's interpretation of this policy is that the institute is afraid that Kin-sey might be retrospectively labelled as a pornographer. But what is lost by gatekeeping material in this way is the possibility for a historical reinterpre-tation, and, in the worst-case scenario, the film material will deteriorate and ultimately disappear for good. In the case of Deutsch's production process, however, the institute discovered it did not own the rights to the particular stag films that he intended to reuse. Based on its exclusive ownership of the (mostly anonymous) source material and a risk assessment, it finally granted him the 'material' permission for reuse. Instead of a licensing fee, it charged him an archival handling fee.

However, the case of rights holders refusing permission for reuse or significantly retarding the process is nothing out of the ordinary. This is the rights owner's prerogative. One example from Deutsch's experience involved an emeritus professor who produced and owned the rights to a medical film that the filmmaker wanted to reuse. There ensued a lengthy exchange of letters between the two, but the rights owner was adamant that he did not want his scientific work reappropriated in an artistic context, and, in the end, Deutsch was forced to look for alternative footage, a situation that Aufderheide and Jaszi (2011, p .1) have termed a 'silent erasure'.

William Wees (1993, p. 11) claims that this sort of scenario is inevitable with found-footage films, as they 'draw attention to the body of the film itself, to the film's own image-ness. [...] [T]hey invite us to recognize it *as* found footage, *as* recycled images'. In their compiled state, the films bring into focus the story that is 'normally' told with the same material. Therefore, in their amalgamated and self-reflexive state, found-footage films are, in many ways, a historiographic intervention – sometimes despite the artists' intentions.

Another example in which the archivists' decisions played a significant role was the production of Peter Delpeut's 1990 film, Lyrisch Nitraat. Delpeut (the deputy director of the Nederlands Filmmuseum at the time of the film's production) was interested in correcting three common misconceptions about early film: he wanted to show that silent films were mostly screened in colour (and not in black and white), exhibit unexpected fluidity when projected at the correct speed (and are not jerky), and do not solely consist of slapstick (they are actually quite 'lyrical') (Delpeut, 2018). Lyrical Nitrate uses EYE's Desmet collection as a hook to tell this story. These silent films, approximately 900 in number, are still part of EYE's collection, and in 2011, they were inscribed in the UNESCO Memory of the World Register. It was common policy in the early 1990s at the Nederlands Filmmuseum to assume that early silent films were not in copyright anymore (Bout, 2017), and so the films in the Desmet collection were considered to be in the public domain. More importantly, however, the Nederlands Filmmuseum was the exclusive owner of the physical material and could restrict access on a material level. When Delpeut made the film, he was still very much on the inside of the archive, and this allowed him to negotiate access to the material. He agreed with the then-director to use only material that had already been preserved, thus limiting his choices at the time of compilation.

Delpeut had privileged access not only to material that had already been preserved, but also to other, less obvious material. In a recent piece, written some 20 years after the film's production, he declares that '[a]ccess is the secret to any documentary' (Delpeut, 2012, p. 223). All the fragments in Lyrisch Nitraat, apart from the closing sequence, originate from the Desmet collection. The spectacular finale shows a random flickering pattern of decaying nitrate, and, according to Delpeut, this scene would never have ended up in the film had he not worked in the film archive – he had simply chanced upon the decomposing scene in the course of his daily archival activities. Despite, or perhaps because of, its advanced state of deterioration, the scene was the only title specifically preserved for his compilation of Lyrisch Nitraat.

Noninstitutional reuse

Found-footage filmmaking can be seen as a practice that keeps 'collections in the public eye and [makes] them matter to modern audiences' (Russell, 2014). In the case of LYRISCH NITRAAT, the Nederlands Filmmuseum, as the institute that housed and owned the nitrate source material helped facilitate access to the historic footage. It also promoted a particular film-historical narrative through its policy of allowing film fragments to be incorporated into newly amalgamated work, thereby highlighting archival lacunae. By writing film history 'with the films themselves' (Fossati, 2012, p. 179), found-footage films continue to pose crucial questions: what is film and, by extension, what is film history? And even, what is the function of the film archive? By attempting to strip films from the history with which they were previously associated, such work foregrounds the concepts of authorship and ownership. The practice of found-footage filmmakers who work outside the institutional archival context, however, brings these questions into even clearer focus.

Traditionally, (analogue) found-footage films have been concerned with 'showcasing the potential of films that have fallen from the mainstream' (de Klerk, 2009, p. 114). Due to the new and innovative ways of accessing more canonical films, current (digital) found-footage practices no longer simply comprise the reuse of leftovers. Several contemporary filmmakers ignore or actively position themselves against the constraints of copyright law: instead of asking permission to reuse material, they have found alternative ways of obtaining their source material, circumventing both archives and rights holders. Arguably, the only manner in which certain films and artworks (that can be seen as 'legally resistant') are now produced is through new, noninstitutional ways of accessing films – examples include Christian Marclay's THE CLOCK (UK 2010), Nicolas Provost's GRAVITY (BE 2007), and Vicky Bennett's THE SOUND OF THE END OF MUSIC (UK 2010).

Marclay, for instance, employed a group of six assistants who watched a plethora of films on DVD that they discovered in a local video store. They captured any scenes that showed clocks or mentioned time in order to provide the artist with a daily selection of new clips (Zalewski, 2012). Provost, at the opening of his retrospective exhibition in Amsterdam in April 2008, claimed that he would never have been able to produce his works had he been dependent on a film archive for his source material, as this would have forced him to obtain permission from rights holders, which was outside of his budget. Like Marclay, he circumvented this by ripping the content off DVDs. Meanwhile, in her presentation at the 'Recycled Film Symposium', held in Newcastle in March 2010, Bennett explained that she initially practiced at a local level – that is, she worked predominantly with educational films and documentaries, most of which originated on VHS. Currently, however, DVDs and broadband internet have enabled her to work with major blockbusters as well.

Marclay, as he had never received a legal objection to any of his previous appropriation art, did not take copyright clearance into consideration when producing THE CLOCK (Zalewski, 2012). On its release, he commented: 'Technically, it's illegal' (*Slave to the Rhythm*, 2010). To date, Marclay has not received any infringement claims, which is perhaps surprising in light of the film's enormous commercial success. Bennett, however, possibly due to her inclusion of a wider array of film material in her work, recently experienced her first legal claim (for THE ZONE) and was forced to withdraw the film from circulation in 2013.[5]

COPYRIGHT EXCEPTIONS

The question of copyright in an artistic context – and of the practices of appropriation art more generally – is a topic worth exploring in more depth; unfortunately, such an investigation lies beyond the scope of this book. However, it is important to briefly discuss at this point the role that copyright exceptions play in enabling the creative reuse of archive material.

UK copyright law provides for a number of exceptions. These are specific circumstances in which the work can be used without the need to get permission from the copyright holder, varying from noncommercial research, education, and private study to quotation, news reporting, parody, and other uses. A number of these exceptions are sometimes referred to as 'fair dealing' exceptions because the law requires that the use of the material for that particular purpose must be what it deems 'fair'. Indeed, each copyright exception has specific requirements about how and when the material can be used without permission, and the filmmaker must satisfy the relevant requirements in order to benefit from it.[6]

Section 30(1ZA) of the Copyright, Designs and Patents Act 1988 (CDPA, 1988) outlines the circumstances in which a work can be quoted: if it has been made available to the public; if the use of the quotation is fair dealing; if the extent of the quotation is no more than is required for its specific purpose; and if the quotation is accompanied by a sufficient acknowledgement (unless this is impractical). The CDPA does not specifically define 'fair dealing'; some factors have been identified by the courts as relevant in deciding whether a particular use is fair, but as the UK Intellectual Property Office (IPO) states, it will always be a matter of fact, degree, and impression in each case.[7]

One relevant factor to consider is the purpose behind using the work: does the material have a different effect than in its original use? Is there a clear connection between the use of the clip and the intention of the larger film? Does it add context or has it been used only for its creative and illustrative value?

Another factor to consider is the proportion of the work that is used. The CDPA does not define what 'no more than is required' means, but it is generally understood as the minimum amount of work that is needed to make a certain point: that is, if a filmmaker wants to quote from someone else's film, he or she must only show a short clip to support their particular argument. However, depending on the circumstances, it may also be fair to quote a particular work in its entirety – for example, if a filmmaker wants to use a photograph for illustrative purposes in a historical documentary, then it may well be fair to show the whole photograph. Thus, in each case, fair dealing is indeed a matter of fact, degree, and impression. The market for the original work is one of the other factors in determining whether a particular use is fair – it is not considered fair if the new work could be seen as a substitute for the original and could affect its commercial exploitation.

Copyright laws differ from country to country. Unlike the UK and most EU countries, US copyright law does not include an exhaustive list of specific copyright exceptions such as quotation or incidental inclusion. However, it does allow fair use of another person's work – a very general and open-ended exception:

> A typical fair use calculation today can be distilled into three questions: Was the use of copyrighted material for a different purpose, rather than just the reuse for the original purpose and for the same audience? [...] Was the amount of material taken appropriate to the purpose of the use? [...] Was it reasonable within the field or discipline it was made in? [...] If the answer to these basic questions is yes, then a court these days - if ever asked - would likely find a fair use. And because that is true, such use is unlikely to be challenged in the first place. (Aufderheide and Jaszi, 2011, pp. 24-25)

If it were tested in the US, Marclay's THE CLOCK would almost certainly be considered fair use. But, as Aufderheide and Jaszi (2011, p. 99) state: 'It is hard to get a test case on fair use, because big companies have good lawyers who see the disadvantages in launching any lawsuit on fair use. Even if they won they would expose the utility of fair use. So they tend to avoid litigation altogether.' In the UK, an argument could be made that the filmmaker could rely on the new exception for quotation. The latter would also possibly be true for Bennett's work.[8]

THE QUESTION OF THE ARCHIVE

David Bordwell has recently argued that different ways of accessing material outside the context of the institutional archive have eradicated the 'economy of scarcity':

> Throughout the 1970s and early 1980s, an economy of scarcity still ruled. Most films, even recent commercial hits, could be found only in studio libraries and public or privately maintained film archives. [...] A procession of new technologies, starting in the 1970s, radically and forever changed access to films, [such as] cable television, [...] VHS, [and] DVD. [...] With so many films easily available on digital formats, people who relied upon archives have found other options. [...] Home video abolished the economy of scarcity. (Bordwell, 2013, pp. 76-78)

While this obviously impacts those in the educational sector, who rely on DVDs to teach film history, it has also affected the contemporary practice of found-footage filmmaking.

In an analogue era, found-footage films made in a public institution were often defined by their noncanonical content and high-quality reproduction. In the case of EYE, Delpeut's LYRISCH NITRAAT (as well as the first two instalments of Deutsch's 'FILM IST' series) can be seen as representative. Outside of this context, however, the alternative ways of obtaining the source material – often of a lesser quality – were ultimately reflected in the final form these films took. A clear example of this aesthetics of access is Müller's HOME STORIES, mentioned above, in which the filmmaker shot 16mm film from a television screen. Another example is Thom Andersen's LOS ANGELES PLAYS ITSELF (US 2003), a video essay about the history of the city's portrayal in film. Andersen (2010) compiled low-resolution video as he was unable to obtain formal permission from the studios to reuse the (Hollywood narrative) film material. Although the filmmaker had been told he would be able to invoke fair use from the time his film was produced, it was only released across home and digital platforms in 2014 after it had been 'remastered with high-definition source material' to Andersen's satisfaction (Wipp, 2014).[9]

In the digital realm, found-footage filmmaking in an institutional context is still often defined by its noncanonical content and the quality of its reproduction, an example being Deutsch's FILM IST. A GIRL & A GUN. However, the films made outside this context have undergone a dramatic transformation; their aesthetics of access are defined on both a formal and a content level. The aforementioned works by Marclay, Provost, and Bennett are all prominent examples: just as in the analogue examples, they draw attention to the body of the film itself, and in a self-reflexive way, the legal provenance of the high-quality Hollywood content has become part of the work itself. By highlighting their provenance, these works could be regarded as resisting their legal restraints.

The practice of found-footage filmmaking has changed greatly over the past few decades. Archives can act as either an impediment or a catalyst to found-footage filmmakers in terms of their ability to access unique material; however, vastly expanded access to video content outside the institutional context has altered their need to work through audiovisual archives. Copyright exceptions and advanced modes of circumvention have made the opposition between institutional and noninstitutional practices more transparent.

Tracing the legal provenance of archival material through the aesthetic form of found-footage films has highlighted the specific interaction between copyright, human agency, and the archive's permission culture. The focus on legal circumvention in found-footage filmmaking – resulting in films that challenge traditional conceptions of authorship and ownership – reveals that the archive's traditional role as the mediator of content may now be at stake.

'BITS & PIECES as synecdoche': A challenge to film history

In light of this scenario, the last part of this chapter highlights how unidentified film fragments, and orphan works more generally, challenge the previously accepted functions of the archival institution: they challenge canonical film history, the role of the film archive in shaping its access-related activities, and the engagement with the 'history making' potential of its holdings. Film fragments in general, and unidentified fragments in particular, defy the classical categories that a film archive (arguably) has to work with:

> The presence of the fragment in the film museum's archives imposes on archivists a hitherto accepted boundary. Exceeding that boundary would challenge their gaze, which is often dominated exclusively by rational categories of written film history. Handling film fragments can thus challenge archivists not only to approach the BITS & PIECES differently but the entire collection. The films should firstly be the subject of pleasure and only secondarily be the subject of identification (and all other related rational activities). This state of affairs can provoke the film archive to approach film history [...] from a more aesthetic point of view rather than from a historical one. Films exist then as the bearer of an affective relationship, and not merely as a historical fact. And as an extension, when screening archival films, they should first be presented as fun and

entertaining facts, and only then as historical ones. Perhaps this would also provoke different choices, other selections in preservation schemes. Perhaps archivists must identify not only with being a custodian and a guardian, but also with being a filmmaker, an *editor* of a beautiful, everlasting film. (Delpeut, 1990, pp. 80-84, author's translation)

In the face of the prevailing rationale of film preservation (part of a general archival culture), the compilation of EYE's Bits & Pieces collection was based overwhelmingly on aesthetic choice – that is, according to the archivist's taste and personal insights. It also led to new ways of presenting the often unusual material, and helped shift the focus away from the established film-historical canon. As Giovanna Fossati (2012, p. 179) notes, the archive has 'always written history by selecting (also by necessity) only a very limited fraction of films to be preserved and presented'. The Nederlands Filmmuseum, however, made the subjectivity of its selection its calling card. In so doing, it challenged the traditional canon – making material available directly influences what can be researched, and the film archive was 'therefore partly responsible for any presuppositions film historians made about the source material' (Lameris, 2017, p. 240).

In her book *The West in Early Cinema, After the Beginning*, Nanna Verhoeff (2006, p. 27) stresses that 'every object found in the archive is a fragment of an irretrievable, ever-widening whole: the "complete" film, the "genre", the program, the cultural habits of watching films, the culture'. As such, the Bits & Pieces collection, she believes, can be seen as a synecdoche (p. 37). She uses the term to mean 'the extension of meaning from bit to whole' (p. 37). In light of the current study's main argument, this figure of speech provides a way of seeing the Bits & Pieces collection as emblematic of the larger group of orphan works and of the whole orphan works problem, which is due to a combination of a specific legality and human agency. Bits & Pieces exposes the gaps in the availability of archival materials, affecting public accessibility to the archive and its potential for contributing to the film-historical narrative.

While the ultimate goal in film restoration is usually to produce a film version that is as complete as possible, by screening the fragments of film in the Bits & Pieces collection, EYE has held up to scrutiny the long-held illusion of the integrity of the archive. The fragments do not only emphasize that a large part of the film archive is in a fragmentary state, but the choice to present the fragments *as* fragments just because they are beautiful challenges both canonical film history (with its focus on complete titles) and the way that film history has been told (ignoring the inevitable lacunae). The reuse of film fragments in found-footage films takes the debate to meta-level: it proposes that multiple, subjective narratives emerge from the archive that are arguably different from the narratives the individual films would have told. BITS & PIECES challenges the whole practice of archival public accessibility.

A significant change in policy and priority has brought about a 'new' archival practice, which valorizes public accessibility and open information, whereby the archive justifies its function by the use of its holdings (Prelinger, 2010). New ways of accessing and using collections have been and are being created by new technologies and new forms of distribution. A particularly current issue is how digitization has provoked a review of archival holdings. Caroline Frick (2011, p. 168) discusses the changing relationship between such concepts as digitization, preservation, and access in an aptly named section of her work called 'Thinking outside the can'. She argues that some regional archives take the approach that digitization *is* preservation and access *is* a form of preservation.

In the late 1970s, classic film history, with its linear macro-histories, shifted to a revisionist stance that focused on nonlinear micro-histories. Just like revisionist film history, which looks for gaps in the historical record, the focus on orphan films brings to the fore lesser-known films, taking into account the role of the archive in not only safeguarding but also actively composing the structure of a certain film-historical narrative. Unidentified film fragments – and orphan works more generally – challenge the institutional role of the film archive, revealing its holdings' potential for 'history making'; they could be seen as an analogy for the potential availability and public accessibility of archival film. The following chapter develops the theme by turning to the larger dynamics of film history.

NOTES

1   An analogy can be discerned in the so-called 'cams' on peer-to-peer platforms, as their aesthetics of access can be linked to their particular distribution platform.

2   Information in this chapter relating to Deutsch's working methods is taken from the (unpublished) transcripts of two semi-structured interviews conducted by the author with the filmmaker. The first one took place in March 2010 in Gorizia, Italy, and the second in April 2010 in New York.

3   Other archives that have preserved fragments and unidentified footage are, for instance, the UCLA Film & Television Archive and the Library of Congress.

4   See: http://www.lesinrocks.com/2000/11/09/musique/techno-au-louvre-11227522/

5   For more information, see https://www.thewire.co.uk/news/22362/vicki-bennett_s-the-zone-withdrawn-from-circulation (accessed on 31 October 2017).

6   This and the following two paragraphs have appeared as part of 'Case File #25, The Accidental Image', written by the author, on the online resource, Copyright User, created by Ronan Deazley and Bartolomeo Meletti. Available at: http://www.copyrightuser.org/educate/the-game-is-on/episode-3-case-file-25/ (accessed on 16 October 2017).

7   See: https://www.gov.uk/guidance/exceptions-to-copyright (accessed on 16 October 2017).

8   Plentiful information about copyright exceptions can be found in Chapter 7 of 'Copyright 101', 'Copyright and Digital Cultural Heritage: Exceptions to Copyright', at the online resource, the Copyright Cortex. Available at: https://copyrightcortex.org/copyright-101/chapter-7 (accessed on 15 October 2017).

9   Perhaps more importantly, the studios would not want to bring a case that they think they would not be able to win, and unwillingly set a precedent. A special thank you to Peter Jaszi for the personal conversations around this topic.

BIBLIOGRAPHY

Andersen, Thom (2010) 'At the Digital Intersection', *Reimagining the Archive: Remapping and Remixing Traditional Models in the Digital Age*, UCLA, Los Angeles, 12–14 November.

Anderson, Steve (2011) *Technologies of History: Visual Media and the Eccentricity of the Past*. Hanover: Dartmouth College Press.

Aufderheide, Patricia and Peter Jaszi (2011) *Reclaiming Fair Use. How to Put Balance Back in Copyright*. Chicago: The University of Chicago Press.

Bandura, Albert (2006) 'Toward a Psychology of Human Agency', *Perspectives on Psychological Science*, 1(2), pp. 164–180. Available at: http://journals.sagepub.com/doi/abs/10.1111/j.1745-6916.2006.00011.x (accessed on 16 October 2017).

Bordwell, David (2013) 'A Celestial Cinémathèque? or, Film Archives and Me: A Semi-Personal History', in Cinémathèque royale de Belgique (ed.) *75000 Films*. Crisnée: Editions Yellow Now, pp. 67–82.

Bout, Leontien (2017) 'Dealing with Orphan Works, a Dutch Film Archive's Perspective', EnDOW publication. Available at: http://diligentsearch.eu/wp-content/uploads/2017/11/L-Bout-presentation-orphan-works-a-film-archives-perspective.pdf (accessed on 9 November 2017).

De Klerk, Nico (2009) 'Designing a Home; Orphan Films in the Work of Gustav Deutsch', in Wilbrig Brainin-Donnenberg and Michael Loebenstein (eds.) *Gustav Deutsch*. Vienna: Filmmuseum Synema Publikationen, pp. 113–122.

Delpeut, Peter (1990) 'Bits & Pieces - De grenzen van het filmarchief', *Versus*, 2, pp. 75–84.

Delpeut, Peter (2012) 'An Unexpected Reception. Lyrical Nitrate Between Film History and Art', in Marente Bloemheuvel, Giovanna Fossati, and Jaap Guldemond (eds.) *Found Footage. Cinema Exposed.* Amsterdam: Amsterdam University Press/EYE Film Institute Netherlands, pp. 218–224.

Delpeut, Peter (2018) 'Prologue. Questions of Colours: Taking Sides', in Giovanna Fossati, Victoria Jackson, Bregt Lameris, Elif Rongen, Sarah Street, and Joshua Yumibe (eds.) *The Colour Fantastic. Chromatic Worlds of Silent Cinema.* Amsterdam: Amsterdam University Press.

Deutsch, Gustav (2010) Interviewed by Claudy Op den Kamp. Gorizia, IT, 22 March.

Deutsch, Gustav (2010) Interviewed by Claudy Op den Kamp. New York, US, 10 April.

Fossati, Giovanna (2012) 'Found Footage. Filmmaking, Film Archiving and New Participatory Platforms', in Marente Bloemheuvel, Giovanna Fossati, and Jaap Guldemond (eds.) *Found Footage. Cinema Exposed.* Amsterdam: Amsterdam University Press/EYE Film Institute Netherlands, pp. 177–184.

Frick, Caroline (2011) *Saving Cinema. The Politics of Preservation.* New York: Oxford University Press.

Habib, André (2006) 'Ruin, Archive and the time of Cinema: Peter Delpeut's *Lyrical Nitrate*', *SubStance* #110, 35(2), pp. 120–139.

Habib, André (2007a) 'Le temps décomposé: ruines et cinéma', Protée, 35(2), pp. 15–26.

Habib, André (2007b) 'Des fragments des premiers temps à l'esthétique de la ruine', in Frank Kessler and Nanna Verhoeff (eds.) *Networks of Entertainment: Early Film Distribution 1895-1915.* Eastleigh: John Libbey, pp. 320-326.

Hausheer, Cecilia, and Christoph Settle (1992) (eds.) *Found Footage Film.* Luzern: Viper/Zyklop Verlag.

Hilderbrand, Lucas (2009) *Inherent Vice: Bootleg Histories of Videotape and Copyright.* Durham: Duke University Press.

Lameris, Bregt (2017) *Film Museum Practice and Film Historiography. The Case of the Nederlands Filmmuseum (1946-2000).* Amsterdam: Amsterdam University Press.

Leyda, Jay (1964) *Films Beget Films. A Study of the Compilation Film.* New York: Hill and Wang.

Prelinger, Rick (2010) 'Points of Origin. Discovering Ourselves Through Access', *The Moving Image*, 9(2), pp. 164–175.

Russell, Patrick (2013) 'Re:found footage', *www.bfi.org.uk* [Online]. Available at: http://www.bfi.org.uk/news-opinion/bfi-news/re-found-footage (accessed on 21 April 2016).

Slave to the rhythm. Christian Marclay on deadline (2010) Available at: http://www.economist.com/node/16885826 (accessed on 16 October 2017)

Thouvenel, Eric (2008) 'How Found Footage Made me Think Twice About Film History', *Cinéma & Cie*, 10, pp. 97–103.

Verhoeff, Nanna (2006) *The West in Early Cinema. After the Beginning*. Amsterdam: Amsterdam University Press.

Wees, William (1993) *Recycled Images: The Art and Politics of Found Footage Films.* New York: Anthology Film Archives.

Wipp, Glenn (2014) '"L.A. PLAYS ITSELF" is finally coming to home video. Here's how', *Los Angeles Times*, 26 July.

Zalewski, Daniel (2012) 'The Hours; How Christian Marclay made the Ultimate Digital Mosaic', *The New Yorker*, 12 March. [Online]. Available at: http://www.newyorker.com/magazine/2012/03/12/the-hours-2 (accessed on 21 April 2016).

ABOUT THE AUTHOR

Claudy Op den Kamp is Lecturer in Film and faculty member at the Centre for Intellectual Property Policy and Management at Bournemouth University, UK, and Adjunct Research Fellow at Swinburne Law School, Australia.

| 131

CHAPTER 6

The Potential for History-Making

Of accidents and activation

Op den Kamp, Claudy, *The Greatest Films Never Seen. The Film Archive* | 133
and the Copyright Smokescreen. Amsterdam University Press, 2018

DOI: 10.5117/9789462981393_CH06

ABSTRACT

This chapter turns to a particular historical example that illustrates how copyright and archival practices have intertwined with one another for as long as film itself has existed.

KEYWORDS
Paper Print Collection, film history, Brighton FIAF Congress 1978, 'activation' of copyright

In the preceding chapters, we explored copyright in relation to archival practices and administrative procedures, highlighting the role human agency plays in these processes. However, before the final chapter draws some conclusions from this analysis, this chapter turns to a particular historical example that illustrates how copyright and archival practices have intertwined with one another for as long as film itself has existed.

This example hails from the formative years of the film industry, a time when (prior to the 1912 Townsend Amendment in US copyright law) motion pictures could not be registered as such for copyright protection. In order to guard their creative products against competitors, filmmakers printed their films onto photographic paper and deposited them for copyright as a series of individual photographs at the US Copyright Office, now collectively known as the Paper Print Collection. This method of complying with a technicality in the copyright law inadvertently led to the preservation of the earliest chapter in US motion picture history – one that would otherwise have been lost to us.

The chapter then goes on to examine the historical significance of the relationship between copyright and archival practices, and some of the consequences of this relationship for the study of film history. It demonstrates not only how (circumventions of) mandatory copyright formalities were instrumental in safeguarding the early film titles, but also how, in turn, the films later played a pivotal role in the landmark 1978 International Federation of Film Archives (FIAF) Congress in Brighton (UK), a crucial turning point in film historiography.

CLOSE-UP: THE PAPER PRINT COLLECTION

The following 'close-up' tells the story of how filmmakers in the US circumvented the early-20th century mandatory copyright formalities, leading to the formation of the Paper Print Collection. The collection (approximately 3000 film titles) was formed in the US Copyright Office at the Library of Congress between 1893 and 1915, where it is still housed today.

The arrival of film is often presented in a somewhat compressed and oversimplified manner, starting with the Lumière Brothers' first public screening (with the first paid admission) in Paris in December 1895.[1] The processes of invention and technological innovation, however, are infinitely more complicated. Film did not arrive as a ready-made invention: the landscape in which it emerged at the end of the nineteenth century was made up of a complex interaction of events and personalities from across the fields of science, technology, art, education, and entertainment (Punt, 2000). The argument that the invention of film was therefore a process that took place over time is borne out by the history of the various experiments in registering the copyright of its early productions.

At the time the new medium was taking shape, around the end of the nineteenth century, US copyright law laid down a series of mandatory formalities, which remained in place until the US became a party to the Berne Convention in 1989.[2] However, the law made no specific provision for motion pictures: celluloid film was still in the process of invention and could not be registered as such. It took time to figure out whether film was an extension of existing media or a new medium that required new regulation. When it was eventually recognized as a medium in its own right, the 1909 US Copyright Act was revised with the Townsend Copyright Amendment in 1912 to allow for the express protection of motion pictures. Peter Decherney (2012, p. 21) argues that the changing methods of applying for copyright 'reflected the battles to define what film [wa]s, and to define standards of originality in filmmaking', and, more importantly, to 'stem the tides of piracy'.

In the US, during the late nineteenth century, Thomas Edison (1894, p. 206) attempted to devise 'an instrument which should do for the eye what the phonograph does for the ear'. Before he entered the film market, however, Edison's work was widely pirated: as his phonograph records were proprietary, they were frequently copied in order to bypass the technologies that tied them to the players (Decherney, 2012). Early film formats were also proprietary: they only fitted with particular devices, preventing an effortless exchange between the discrete apparatuses. Sprocket holes, for instance, were located in different places on the actual film strips. The lack of standardization was an important motivation behind early film-copying practices: only by re-photographing each film frame – known as 'duping' – could these proprietary systems be copied into each other. But it was not merely a lack of standardization that led to the duping of existing films, an arguably more important reason was the fact that it was less expensive than producing an original film. Sometimes films were copied one-to-one and resold as such, sometimes they would be copied, recut, and sold as a new story under a new name. In order to avoid a repetition of his previous experiences with the phonograph, Edison devised innovative ways to protect his work against competitors, one of which he appears to have discovered by chance.[3]

In order to illustrate his company's new motion picture technology for a promotional article in *Harper's Weekly*, Edison exposed the negative for a Kinetoscopic Record of a Sneeze on strips of bromide photographic contact paper and affixed them to a cardboard backing. Decherney (2012) argues that it must have occurred to someone that they had transformed a film into an object that could be protected by copyright. Edison's assistant W.K.L. Dickson sent the object to the Copyright Office to be registered – not as a *film* but as a *photograph*. EDISON KINETOSCOPIC RECORD OF A SNEEZE shows one of Edison's engineers, Fred Ott, inhaling some snuff and then sneezing violently (hence, the piece is colloquially known as FRED OTT'S SNEEZE); it is the first surviving paper print at the Library of Congress, dated January 1894.[4]

So it was that a chain of historical 'accidents', which must have seemed of little significance at the time, were crucial to the formation of the Paper Print Collection. First, a clerk at the Copyright Office decided that the paper print could be registered as a photograph (Mashon, 2013); moreover, the paper print was not just registered as a photograph, but a *series* of photographs were registered as *one* photograph. Second, although there were experiments with other registration methods, such as registering representative frames of each scene of a film,[5] the practice of registering films as photographs went unchallenged for nearly a decade. Third, the paper prints were handled in much the same way as other Library of Congress registration records: they were filed and put into storage in the basement of the Library's Jefferson building. Finally, upon opening the basement door many years later, someone saw the potential worth of what they found there and made a case for the prints' revival (Walls, 1953; Loughney, 1988; Grimm, 1999; Paletz, 2001).

There is yet another historical accident that should not be overlooked in the larger story of the Paper Print Collection. Around 1915, actual motion pictures began to be registered, but, because of the inflammable nature of the nitrate stock, they were photographed and printed on, the decision was made *not* to keep these films. This policy changed in the late 1940s when the Library of Congress acquired appropriate storage facilities for the inflammable nitrate material (Mashon, 2013). As a consequence, the library initially contained a wealth of film material from before 1912 but little from 1912 to the late 1940s. Undoubtedly, there were many more such moments that carried an unanticipated significance for the formation and survival of the collection.

The rediscovery of the Paper Print Collection is another story replete with serendipitous connections, this time involving both credited and uncredited contributors.[6] It encompasses voluntary contributions to the collection's initial compilation of an inventory; grant applications for restoration; external collaborations with other film archives, such as the UCLA Film Archive[7] and the Academy of Motion Picture Arts & Sciences; and a special Academy award for the collection's restoration efforts. Unlike the (lost) films from which they were copied, the paper prints could not be projected, but had to be copied back onto film. As they had been kept rolled up for several decades, it was necessary first to restore their pliability – a process that was complicated by the early equipment's lack of standardization. This account cannot detail the frame-by-frame restoration of the 2.5 million feet of paper rolls, as the main focus here is on some of the legal concerns affecting the public accessibility of archival material, but it is important to note that issues of restoration also play a part in impeding or facilitating access to the film material.

This section can only give a glimpse of the richness of the Paper Print Collection's contents.[8] The collection not only illuminates a pioneering chapter of film history, with the earliest examples of 'actualities' (documentaries showing everyday life), preserving an astonishing record of American industrial life at the turn of the 20th century, but it also provides an exceptional insight into the evolution of narrative film. It contains examples of the development of film from what Tom Gunning (1990, pp. 232-233) has termed the 'cinema of attraction' through to its 'narrativization' in the first few decades of the 1900s. Highlights of the collection include such landmark films as Edwin S. Porter's THE GREAT TRAIN ROBBERY (US 1903), widely considered to be one of the first Westerns, as well as a significant part of the oeuvre of filmmaker D.W. Griffith.

It is worth restating at this point that it is of course only possible to study films if they have survived and are (made) publicly accessible, and this has an obvious effect on film history. *Film history* is generally understood as the history of films, whereas *cinema history* is the history of film's relation to society or culture (Punt, 2000; Strauven, 2013). Cinema history can be told without the films themselves – for instance, through architectural records, patent registrations, and trade papers. Film history can also be told without the films, but once we focus on a critical understanding of the more aesthetic side of the story, such as the development of (continuity) editing, the study of film form, or the evolution of storytelling, the films themselves have to play a key role. An individual researcher can of course consult a large majority of titles on the premises of an archive; however, what is at stake here is the wider accessibility of films that is crucial to constructing more comprehensive frameworks of meaning.

Following initial restoration efforts, film prints of some of the titles first started to become available in the late 1960s; they began to circulate among libraries and universities as 16mm compilations (Bordwell, 1997). The films went on to become a staple of the American avant-garde in the 1960s and 1970s: filmmakers such as Ken Jacobs, Hollis Frampton, and Ernie Gehr reused films from the Paper Print Collection in their artworks in the process of interrogating and exploring the different dimensions of narrative, authorship, and ownership (Testa, 1992). The films also played a fundamental role as primary source material in the FIAF Brighton Congress in 1978 (briefly mentioned in Chapter 1). Both the archival and the academic film communities view this conference as the cornerstone of what has come to be known as the 'New Film History' (Chapman, Glancy, and Harper, 2007).

The Brighton Congress was a groundbreaking collaborative venture between archivists and film scholars, who were gathered together as a group for the first time. Over the course of several days, they watched hundreds of fiction films, in chronological order, from the period between 1900 and 1906. Prior to the Brighton Congress, film history had generally consisted of recording handed-down recollections: 'Georges Sadoul, Jean Mitry, and other postwar historians [...] wrote their vast tomes on the basis of [...] memories, not intensive [...] viewing' (Bordwell, 2013, p. 73). The so-called New Film Historians who emerged from the Congress questioned the sources of their predecessors, as well as the particular use of those sources. By contrast, their aim was to return to the archival films, using them as a primary source with which to challenge previously unquestioned notions about film itself. This project entailed, on the one hand, a revision of already familiar material, and, on the other, a wider exploration of the film archives in search of uncharted material.[9]

The films shown during the Congress were provided by several large international archival institutions, such as the Museum of Modern Art, but, by far, the largest number was supplied by the Library of Congress from the archive of films submitted for copyright to the Paper Print Collection (Bowser, 1979). The screenings and the subsequent scholarship led to a fundamental reevaluation and revision of the early silent film period. Of course, the oeuvres of later individual filmmakers, such as Alfred Hitchcock or Howard Hawks, have been revised over the years, but no other major period in film history has been subjected to so systematic a revision based on the available filmic source material. The new approach to history – based on actually *watching* the films – changed the conception of the film archive from *terra incognita* to a repository of historical artefacts and filmic source material.

It is now (at the time of writing) a little over 120 years since Fred Ott's sneeze was captured on film, and it has recently been added to the National Film Registry (Barnes, 2015) – a list, started in 1989 (see Chapter 2), which each year adds a further 25 films deemed to be of outstanding cultural, historic, or artistic value. Although, at the time of the prints' rediscovery in the early 1940s, they struggled to 'transcend individual estimations of their significance as history' (Paletz, 2001, p. 79), there is now little doubt that the oldest surviving paper print has true historic worth.

Thus, an 'ingenious method of complying with a technicality in the copyright law [...] became the inadvertent means for recovering film history' (Paletz, 2001, p. 71). But the story of the Paper Print Collection continues to be a work-in-progress. Film preservation is never done. The discovery and recovery of film history is similarly a continuing story of cultural reinterpretation. John Arnold (2000, p. 122) argues that 'history is an argument, and arguments present the opportunity for *change*'. Despite ongoing digitization efforts, less than 20% of the collection is widely accessible for viewing: some 500 titles are available online, while currently all the other titles of the collection have to be consulted in Washington.[10] Only if it is publicly accessible, can this material provide the opportunity for debate and argument, for reassessing, revising, and writing history.

THEMES AND TENSIONS

There are three components in the story of the Paper Print Collection that are of particular interest in light of the larger relationship addressed in this book between the film archive, copyright, and film historiography: (1) the historical accidents that take place in archival practice, which can be called the 'activation of IP'; (2) the public domain status of the collection at the moment of its reuse; and (3) the public accessibility of the material that leads to the films' potential for history-making, including reinterpretations of what has gone before.

| 139

1. Archival practice, and the 'activation of copyright'

Archival access is not only controlled by those who own the rights, but also by those who own the physical assets. As argued earlier, copyright is a guiding filter for digitization and archival access practices, and is enhanced by certain key factors inherent to institutional archival practice, including the active choices of its archivists. Human agency is clearly expressed in the example of the Paper Print Collection: someone decided that a series of photographs could be registered for copyright as a single photograph; someone decided *not* to keep the nitrate film copies once it was possible to deposit celluloid for copyright; and someone fought for the films' restoration. This 'activation of copyright' can be discerned particularly within the confines of an archival institution.

2. Public domain status

Mandatory copyright formalities have been instrumental in the preservation of the earliest chapter in US film history. The legal context in which the films emerged, however, is only part of the story. The copyright status of the material at the moment of its reuse (public domain) plays a vital role in the films' wider accessibility for further study, and is perhaps as important as their fascinating content.

As the two examples of the reuse of films from the Paper Print Collection (mentioned earlier) show, their public domain status was a crucial yet far less acknowledged catalyst in the events. Aside from the use of their marvelous content for *détournement*, the importance of found-footage films to the American avant-garde movement was partially economic: there was no need for a camera and no costs attached to purchasing or processing the films, so the budget could be relatively low. There were also no costs for copyright permissions in the case of the Paper Print Collection, as these films were in the public domain. The same applied to the films screened at the FIAF Brighton Congress. The Congress has often been framed in revisionist terms in its relation to early cinema.[11] But film researchers and legal scholars alike have failed to notice the crucial role that the copyright status of the film material plays in the process. The systematic revision of a particular period of film history was undertaken with the material that was easiest to use, legally speaking; the same sort of revision of periods still under copyright would be significantly harder to prepare and organize.

3. The potential for (film) history-making

What the example of the Paper Print Collection makes clear is that film history is composed of archival lacunae: any films that survived were registered for copyright, but it is not hard to imagine that there must have been many more films produced. The collection represents the so-called 'survivors of film history' (Mashon, 2013). There is no accurate record of how many films were produced during the earliest days of film, nor is it known what particular percentage survives worldwide.[12] The Paper Print Collection itself represents a significant portion of the percentage of titles that survived in the US. However, we can only study those films that survive if they are publicly accessible. Some of the filmmakers and companies that are well-represented in the collection can be studied simply because their material is available, and, as a result, we tend to endow it with qualities that are possibly erroneous – for example, the reason there appear to be so many 'firsts' in the collection is undoubtedly due to the fact that it is the only material that is available.

What the example of the Paper Print Collection also makes clear (partially through the exposure of its archival lacunae) is that it is essential to take a critical stance towards source material. This is perhaps even more the case at present, a time of seemingly ubiquitous access, when the landscape of the place of storage for filmic sources is changing in response to digitization and funding pressures. Placing the source material in its historical context – understanding what factors influence its accessibility, including its legal provenance – is crucial to the analysis of that part of the archival collection that is publicly accessible.

The creation of the Paper Print Collection was due not to the mandatory copyright formalities, but to their circumvention. Over several decades, the films have shifted in nature from registration records to historical artefacts and primary source material for film-historical research. It was the legal context and copyright status of the material, plus the human agency behind the 'activation of IP' during the process of circumvention that allowed the film material to express its potential for further history-making. Thus, the material itself embodies the history of copyright *in relation to* archival practices and administrative procedures. The example of the Paper Print Collection confirms that, when copyright is used to analyze public access, it helps bring to light these archival practices, and (paradoxically) shifts the focus of the debate away from an exclusively legal one.

Although archives, and particularly public-sector archives, are essential to the safeguarding and preservation of film material, they are not neutral institutions. Extant material is not necessarily available and available material is not necessarily publicly accessible. A certain fragmentation takes place in the archive that results in a narrow(er) and fragmentary view of its holdings, and, as such, the archive can be seen as a mediator between copyright and the potential for history-making.

THE ARCHIVE AND 'DOING' HISTORY

The films in the Paper Print Collection played a paramount role in the New Film History. These revisionist historians criticized the chronology and teleology of traditional historiography, whose main topic was the 'history of film as a progressive development from simpler to more complex forms, treated according to that biological analogy of birth/childhood/maturity' (Bordwell, 1997, p. 9). Classical film history was therefore based on the assumption that a succession of individual filmmakers were responsible for the evolution of film in an orderly and linear fashion into an increasingly nuanced art form, and the resulting historiography comprised a description of creative movements associated with directors and their masterpieces. In radical contrast to this, the New Film Historians aimed to study film 'from its own point of view, not simply as part of an evolutionary scheme' (Horak, Lacasse, and Cherchi Usai, 1991, p. 282).

These historians also questioned the material sources their predecessors based their histories on, as well as their use of those sources: what marks out New Film History is its call for a return to archival primary sources, both filmic and (specifically) non-filmic. Up to the late 1970s, however, one of the greatest difficulties was the lack of material available for intensive viewing. David Bordwell (2013, p. 68) states that, partly due to the nature of the material, '[f]or about eighty years, the study of film history was dominated by an economy of scarcity'. Consequently, the writing of film history traditionally comprised a theoretical reconstruction without recourse to the material evidence of the films themselves; it was based instead mainly on catalogues, clippings, and recollections. The call for primary research, however, precipitated a return to the material filmic sources (Elsaesser, 1986). In a transcript of a roundtable discussion ten years after the Brighton Congress, Tom Gunning highlights the conference's importance in this respect – and the excitement it generated:

> The exciting thing for me [...] was the possibility of really seeing the films, for a period that was largely legendary. It was covered in almost every basic history, but often these histories, particularly the ones available in English, were several decades old. [...] [T]he importance of looking at the films themselves [...] was equally important to working out production histories and social histories. To actually look at the films themselves and to understand how they were operating became in many ways the most crucial focus of the new work. (Gunning, cited in Horak, Lacasse and Cherchi Usai, 1991, p. 282)

The emphasis on the reevaluation of existing histories was corroborated by Jan-Christopher Horak in the same roundtable discussion:

> When I think back on Brighton it seems [...] important just in terms of my view of film history. Having previously been to graduate school, where even though there was a concentration on film and film history, you really only saw the canon of film history, which meant you got to see, at best, a few Meliès, a Lumière or two, THE GREAT TRAIN ROBBERY, maybe LIFE OF AN AMERICAN FIREMAN (the old version), and that was about it. And here, for the first time you got not a horizontal view into film history, but really first vertical and then horizontal in a way that has changed my thinking completely on the history of cinema. It's had an enormous impact, because

for me the term primitive cinema is no longer a part of my vocabulary since Brighton. (Horak in Horak, Lacasse, and Cherchi Usai, 1991, p. 283)

Horak also underlines how the event's remit crucially included the attempt to identify historical gaps, to indicate the importance of films previously considered insignificant, and potentially to discover archival rarities through an exploration of the uncharted territory of the film archive:

> [I]t made me realise that if it's true for this early period, it was probably true for every period of film history. You could learn from every kind of film, whether it was the worst trash, or a film that was considered high art, because here we were looking at a period that, according to the classic historians, was in fact not worth considering at all, and we were finding all these gems. And I think that just that change in the attitude towards film history, was a very important experience. (Horak in Horak, Lacasse and Cherchi Usai, 1991, p. 283)

As James Chapman, Mark Glancy, and Sue Harper (2007, p. 7) claim, the revisionist film history's call for primary research also 'expanded the range of primary sources available to the researcher'. For example, there was a renewed focus on different kinds of sources – that is, other, previously ignored non-filmic primary sources, such as patent registrations or architectural records, that could potentially shed light on the history of film. In his landmark essay, 'Writing the History of the American Film Industry: Warner Bros and Sound', dating from just before the Brighton Congress, Douglas Gomery states:

> [W]e must not simply trust the old bibliographies or faulty recollections, but go out and seek the evidence wherever it may be. [...] We must [...] begin to search out new sources of primary data [...] to challenge the usual conclusion, as well as the terms in which that explanation is written. (Gomery, 1976, p. 119)

The New Film Historians were interested in revealing the existence of different kinds of histories, other than that of the 'masterpiece tradition', as Robert Allen and Douglas Gomery (1985, p. 71) call canonical film history. These other histories included the history of film technology and of film's relationship with society or culture. The renewed focus on non-filmic sources, the 'contextual aspects of film history beyond the film artefact' (Gosvig Olesen, 2017, p. 76), led to a new discipline, *cinema history* – that is, 'the history of cinema as institution, as exhibition practice, as social space (as opposed to *film history*, which is, generally speaking, a history of masters and masterpieces)'

(Strauven, 2013, p. 5). As recently as 1975, film history was considered to be the history of films, and it was written as if films had no audience or were seen by everyone in the same way (Kuhn and Stacey, 1998). But, as Thomas Elsaesser (1986, p. 248) says, '[t]o do film history today, one has to become an economic historian, a legal expert, a sociologist, an architectural historian, know about censorship and fiscal policy, read trade papers and fan magazines'.

One final but key point in which the New Film Historians differed from their predecessors was their collaboration with film archives and archivists, a result of their newfound interest for archival sources. Former Museum of Modern Art film curator John Gartenberg argues:

> [T]he scholars' awareness about materials held [was limited]. On their part, researchers have often relied on their memories and secondary sources, including other written film histories, rather than digging into primary resource materials in the archives. [...] Scholars have often viewed archivists as unnecessarily secretive about their holdings. Conversely, archivists have viewed scholars as largely unaware of the workings of a film archive and of the delicate role the archivists play as mediators between the owners of the films [...] and the users of the product. This kind of collaboration between film archives and universities and archivists and film scholars is significant not only for the recent Brighton publication, but also in the model it established for future interactions on similar such projects involving intense study of neglected areas of film history. (Gartenberg, 1984, pp. 6-13)

FIAF Brighton was the first time that archivists intervened in film history by curating a film programme that allowed film historians to draw new conclusions. This changed the relationship between academics and archivists from a vendor-client one to a cooperative venture. The Orphan Film Symposium, a biannual gathering of film scholars and archivists with the aim of studying 'all manner of films outside the commercial mainstream',[13] is a contemporary example of this sort of collaboration. This gathering focuses on viewing these films (in a revisionist spirit) in order to study neglected areas of film history.

Thus, the availability and public accessibility of archival film material remains a topical concern:

> [T]he Brighton meeting was itself symptomatic of a new urgency felt by film archives about the preservation and accessibility of materials from the early period. [...] As so often in historiography, new criteria of pertinence necessarily affect the hypotheses historians forge, consciously or unconsciously, about the data in question. (Elsaesser, 1990, pp. 2-3)

144

In the context of the film archive, this means that different stories can be told using the same body of work. Perhaps more importantly, a different kind of film history to that of the canonical textbook variety emerges when the researcher takes into consideration the archive's material holdings. The primary source material can be used for reinterpretations, arguments, and opportunities for change – in short, it holds the potential for history-making.

Canonical film history is driven by the notion that only a small portion of all films is worthy of serious study. But, as we saw earlier, there is often a serious discrepancy between textbook film history and the actual holdings of an archive. In many ways, the New Film Historians, in their 'return to the archive', rejected the whole notion of a canon as a central guide to writing history. The film archive itself is a testament to the fact that the records that survive into the present are always incomplete: it is impossible to collect everything that has been produced, and it is impossible to preserve everything that has been collected. The problem is that the sheer volume and quality of the world's film archives – from national institutions (such as EYE) to local and private collections – conveys a sense of archival completeness. Recently, this misleading impression has, to some extent, been exacerbated by developments in digitization and a shift in focus towards digital access.

In the preceding chapters, we looked at copyright ownership as one of the factors impacting archival access. Other factors include the institutional context of the archive, and its acquisition policies and preservation activities. The process of digitization of analogue material – the migration of digital files, the creation of video masters in different sorts of formats (ranging from cinema projection to streaming), and ensuring the formats are compatible – is a costly affair. Hence, funding issues, especially when the investment in preservation is tied to providing online access, have become arguably the most fundamental impediment to access.

In this context, it is worth revisiting some of the archival practices and administrative procedures that underpin the fragmentation of the archive. Film historians construct a version of film history based on those films that film museums have collected, restored, and provided access to over the course of the years (Lameris, 2007). This visible part of the archive, however, is only part of the picture; for various reasons, be they political, economic, or curatorial, 'historians are not seeing most of the films that exist to be studied' (Streible, 2009, p. ix). Indeed, in 2000, Paolo Cherchi Usai (p. 69) claimed that 'less than 5 percent of all the film titles preserved in the average film archive is seen by scholars [...] and much of the remaining 95 percent never leaves the shelves of the film vaults after preservation has been completed'. More recently, Janna Jones (2012) has chronicled how current preservation practices help shape cinematic heritage. She echoes Allen and Gomery (1985) when she highlights certain 'masterpiece' restoration practices and addresses what can be seen as a process of canonization within the archival practice:

> Archives do have a relatively small collection of archival gems that they rely upon to help commemorate and acknowledge the cinematic past, but they do not have the time or the money to construct identities and cinematic meanings for most of their material. [...] Until an archive can construct frameworks of meaning, moving images are merely celluloid matter that requires care and maintenance. Cinematic abundance suggests potential for the writing of future histories, but most unidentified film cannot speak for itself. Filmic material cannot reach its potential for history making until its biography unfolds. [...] It is often the case that the materials with an already stable identity receive the most attention and their biographies continue to grow. [...] Films deemed important by the archive circulate more easily, helping to reify their cultural and historical meanings. Films that have not yet been considered for preservation tend to remain obscure and unseen. [...] Current restoration discourse and practices literally assemble and help to shape cinematic history and reveal how the moving image archive influences the ways that a film history is understood. (Jones, 2012, pp. 112-137)

As Ian Christie (2013, p. 42) observes, this process of canonization is 'self-reinforcing, since canonic works tend to be shown most often, to be selected for restoration by archives, and to be used in education'. However, Bordwell (2013, p. 81) has recently suggested that the canon has 'largely collapsed' and that 'there are no longer "minor" films. Every movie is potentially an object of veneration for some audience, and an answer to some research question. [...] [T]he economy of scarcity has become an economy of glut.' Archives still 'harbor a great many uncelebrated films that can shed light on the history of cinema art. If you are asking certain questions, no film is uninteresting' (p. 68).

New technologies have been and are being created to use and distribute collections in new ways, leading to heightened expectations of accessible collections that are 'universal, instant, online, and free' (Enticknap, 2007, p. 15). Chapter 4 also looked at issues of digitization, in particular the 'digital skew' (the disparity between analogue and digitized collections) in relation to works in the public domain. The issue of what could be called a 'cultural skew' is obviously far larger than the case of the public domain works suggests. As Horak (2007, p. 30; p. 40) states, only a 'minute amount of material in relation to the total holdings of public archives has been digitized. [...] [T]he rest remains invisible to all but a handful of specialists.' In 2007, 82% of the National Film Registry was not available to general audiences in any digital format (Horak,

2007, p. 39). This percentage includes silent films, documentaries, avant-garde films, and independent films by ethnic minorities. Their unavailability has an immediate effect on the ways in which these sources can be used:

> This limited access to our collective film history severely constricts the scope of what can be taught to students now that the majority of college faculty teach primarily from DVDs. Thus, the construction of film courses is increasingly limited to a canon according to the market logic of Block-buster Video. [...] Given these restrictions, students are confronted with a fragmented, incomplete, and distorted view of film history, based on what commercial distributors deem to be viable in the marketplace rather than what scholarship has ascertained as important. (Horak, 2007, p. 39)

This relatively limited range of available archival sources not only impacts teaching, especially the teaching of film history, but also has more long-term consequences for historical research, and the construction of the history of film that relies on these sources, and film historiography.

THE 'RESEARCH PROGRAM'

'The basic problems about "doing" film history are the same as with any other form of history: what is the object of study, what counts as evidence and, finally, what is being explained?' (Elsaesser, 1986, p. 247) Paul Grainge, Mark Jancovich, and Sharon Monteith describe the challenge of film-historical research as follows:

> Research is always about finding a focus. The attempt to capture and reproduce the richness and fullness of the historical past is not only impossible but seeks to mirror its object of study, rather than identify a purpose for studying it and studying what is relevant or irrelevant to that purpose. As a result, the intense conflicts over the relevance and irrele-vance of specific details, or over what is significant, is not simply a conflict over absences or omissions but over the appropriate focus and purpose of historical research. (Grainge, Jancovich, and Monteith, 2007, p. x)

David Bordwell and Kristin Thompson (1994, p. xxxiii) call the particular fram-ing of the film-historical enquiry the 'research program and its questions'. This term moves the focus away from a desire for historical 'completeness' to the critical framing that is expressed in the historian's deliberate choices as he or she is (of necessity) forced to select from a wealth of material.

Written history always requires the intervention of a human interpreter (Manoff, 2004), and, as a result, it is a process that will always be partial, provisional, and written from the viewpoint of the present. For this reason, the most interesting histories are those that challenge the usual conclusions. Christian Keathley (2006) claims that Thomas Elsaesser was one of the first historians to encourage the exploration of so-called counterfactual film histories. Counterfactual history is a form of historiography that pursues the *what if* questions: that is, 'histories that would mine undeveloped or unconsidered points of entry into the cinema as object of study' (Keathley, 2006, p. 133). According to Elsaesser (cited in Keathley, 2006, p. 134), '[s]uch a counter-factual conception of history is not the opposite of a "real" history, but a view prepared to think into history all those histories that might have been, or might still be'.

Both the 1978 Brighton Congress and the Nederlands Filmmuseum, which, in the late 1980s and early 1990s began to focus on the aesthetics of its own archival collection instead of following established historical categories, are examples of events or policies that led to the rewriting of history and the birth of counterfactual film histories. Both examples asked the question *what if*? In the case of the Brighton Congress, the main question underpinning the endeavour to screen as many surviving fiction films from 1900 to 1906 as possible was: what if the actual films are screened, viewed, and examined? Will they upturn accepted notions of this so-called 'primitive' period of cinema? Whereas the question the Nederlands Filmmuseum posed was: what if the preservation and presentation of the archive's collection is based on the archivists' personal understanding of what is beautiful or pleasurable (in contrast to the focus of other institutions)? How will this impact the established canon of film?

When the same material is 'reshuffled', a different story emerges, and a new point of entry into cinema as an object of study appears, and when the usual conclusions based on archival sources are challenged, their true potential for history-making is revealed.

NOTES

1   As recently as 2011, the invention of cinema was portrayed this way in Martin Scorsese's HUGO (US, Paramount Pictures).
2   During the 1908 Berlin Revision of the Berne Convention, mandatory copyright formalities, such as registration, renewal, notice, and deposit, were abolished. They were gradually eliminated in all the signatory countries and copyright protection nowadays is automatic upon creation, and exists separately of formalities.

3   A more detailed account of the period remains outside the scope of this book. For an excellent examination of the period, see Peter Decherney (2012). Pascal Kamina (2016) states that films raised *two* series of questions in terms of copyright protection. The first concerned the protection of films against infringement by competitors and unlicensed theatre owners; the second, the possibility of infringing preexisting works, mainly novels or dramas, through cinematography. The second concern, however fascinating, also remains outside the scope of this book.

4   The production date of the film is 7 January 1894; the copyright registration date is 9 January 1894.

5   In comparison, the British Film Copyright Collection consists entirely of individual frame enlargements and representative frames of each scene. It cannot be used for the study of film (form) in the way that the US Paper Print Collection can be used. The UK frames are the only surviving records of the subjects and researchers have unearthed the names of some previously unknown producers. The 'collection' has mainly been used to correct information about dates, titles, and names. For more background on the British Collection, see Richard Brown (1996).

6   Whether the discovery of the collection should be called a 'discovery' at all is open for debate. Although there is some evidence that Library of Congress staff knew that these artefacts were in the library's basement, nothing was really ever done with them (Grimm, 1999). What is important to note in this context, however, is that, when the titles were rediscovered and reused (depending on which precise date is chosen), they had already fallen into the public domain. This information was provided by Mike Mashon in a personal email to the author on 27 August 2015.

7   This is now the UCLA Film & Television Archive.

8   For a descriptive analysis of the collection, see Patrick Loughney (1988).

9   The issue of demand is also discernible here: until film historians began reevaluating early film history, there was virtually no interest in these films, and therefore there was no institutional will to preserve them or make them accessible.

10 Available at: http://blogs.loc.gov/now-see-hear/2014/05/where-it-all-began-the-paper-print-collection/ The other titles can be consulted at the Motion Picture Television Reading Room, Motion Picture, Broadcasting and Recorded Sound Division, Library of Congress, Washington, DC (accessed on 18 October 2017).

11 A recent point of historiographic interest is that the material of the screenings in black and white at the Conference, 'which had so energetically revamped the study of early cinema, had originally been in colour' (Delpeut, 2018, p. 25).

12 David Pierce (2013) has meticulously researched the survival rate in the American context.

13 Available at: http://www.nyu.edu/orphanfilm/ (accessed on 23 April 2016).

BIBLIOGRAPHY

Arnold, John (2000) *History. A Very Short Introduction*. Oxford: Oxford University Press.

Barnes, Mike (2015) '"GHOSTBUSTERS", "TOP GUN", "SHAWSHANK" Enter National Film Registry', *Hollywood Reporter*, 16 December [Online]. Available at: http://www.hollywoodreporter.com/news/ghostbusters-top-gun-enter-national-849092 (accessed on 22 January 2016)

Bordwell, David (1997) *On the History of Film Style*. Cambridge: Harvard University Press.

Bordwell, David (2013) 'A Celestial Cinémathèque? or, Film Archives and Me: A Semi-Personal History', in Cinémathèque royale de Belgique (ed.) *75000 Films*. Crisnée: Editions Yellow Now, pp. 67–82.

Bordwell, David, and Kristin Thompson (1994) *Film History. An Introduction*. New York: McGraw-Hill.

Bowser, Eileen (1979) 'The Brighton Project: An Introduction', *Quarterly Review of Film Studies*, 4(4), pp. 509–538.

Brown, Richard (1996) 'The British Film Copyright Archive', in Colin Harding and Simon Popple (eds.) *In the Kingdom of Shadows: Companion to Early Cinema*. London: Cygnus Arts, pp. 240–245.

Chapman, James, Mark Glancy, and Sue Harper (eds.) (2007) *The New Film History. Sources, Methods, Approaches*. Basingstoke: Palgrave Macmillan.

Cherchi Usai, Paolo (2000) *Silent Cinema: An Introduction*. London: British Film Institute.

Christie, Ian (2013) 'New Lamps for Old: What Can we Expect From Archival Film Festivals?', in Alex Marlow-Mann (ed.) *Film Festival Yearbook 5: Archival Film Festivals*. St Andrews: St Andrews Film Studies, pp. 41–53.

Decherney, Peter (2012) *Hollywood Copyright Wars*. New York: Columbia University Press.

Delpeut, Peter (2018) 'Prologue. Questions of Colours: Taking Sides', in Giovanna Fossati, Victoria Jackson, Bregt Lameris, Elif Rongen, Sarah Street, and Joshua Yumibe (eds.) *The Colour Fantastic. Chromatic Worlds of Silent Cinema*. Amsterdam: Amsterdam University Press.

Edison, Thomas (1894) 'Edison's Invention of the Kineto-Phonograph', *The Century, A Popular Quarterly*, 48(2), pp. 206–214.

Elsaesser, Thomas (1986) 'The New Film History', *Sight & Sound*, 55(4), pp. 246–251.

Elsaesser, Thomas (ed.) (1990) *Early Cinema. Space, Frame, Narrative*. London: British Film Institute.

Enticknap, Leo (2007) 'Have Digital Technologies Reopened the Lindgren/Langlois Debate?', *Spectator*, 27(1), pp. 10–20.

Gartenberg, John (1984) 'The Brighton Project: Archives and Historians', *IRIS*, 2(1), pp. 5–16.

Gomery, Douglas (1985 [1976]) 'Writing the History of the American Film Industry: Warner Brothers and Sound', in Bill Nichols (ed.) *Movies and Methods: An Anthology. Volume II*. Berkeley and Los Angeles: University of California Press, pp. 109–120.

Grainge, Paul, Mark Jancovich, and Sharon Monteith (eds.) (2007) *Film Histories. An Introduction and Reader*. Toronto and Buffalo: University of Toronto Press.

Grimm, Charles (1999) 'A Paper Print Pre-History', *Film History*, 11(2), pp. 204–216.

Gunning, Tom (1990) 'The Cinema of Attraction: Early Film, Its Spectator and the Avant-Garde', in Thomas Elsaesser (ed.) *Early Cinema. Space, Frame, Narrative*. London: British Film Institute, pp. 229-235.

Horak, Jan-Christopher (2007) 'The Gap Between 1 and 0: Digital Video and the Omissions of Film History', *Spectator*, 27(1), pp. 29–41.

Horak, Jan-Christopher, Alain Lacasse, and Paolo Cherchi Usai (1991) 'FIAF Conference, Lisbon, 1989: The Brighton FIAF Conference (1978): Ten Years After', *Historical Journal of Film, Radio & Television,* 11(3), pp. 279–292.

Jones, Janna (2012) *The Past is a Moving Picture. Preserving the Twentieth Century on Film*. Gainesville: University Press of Florida.

Kamina, Pascal (2016) *Film Copyright in the European Union*. Cambridge: Cambridge University Press.

Keathley, Christian (2006) *Cinephilia and History, or the Wind in the Trees*. Bloomington: Indiana University Press.

Kuhn, Annette, and Jackie Stacey (1998) (eds.) *Screen Histories. A Screen Reader*. Oxford: Clarendon Press.

Lameris, Bregt (2007) *Opnieuw belicht: de pas de deux tussen de filmmuseale praktijk en filmhistorische debatten*. PhD Dissertation, Universiteit Utrecht.

Loughney, Patrick (1988) *A Descriptive Analysis of the Library of Congress Paper Print Collection and Related Copyright Materials*. PhD Dissertation, George Washington University.

Manoff, Marlene (2004) 'Theories of the Archive from Across the Disciplines', *Libraries and the Academy*, 4(1), pp. 9–25.

Mashon, Mike (2013) 'Early Motion Pictures', *American Artifacts*, C-SPAN, 27 March [Online] Available at: http://www.c-span.org/video/?313371-1/early-motion-pictures (accessed on 12 November 2015).

Olesen, Christian Gosvig (2017) *Film History in the Making. Film Historiography, Digitised Archives and Digital Research Dispositifs*. PhD Dissertation, University of Amsterdam.

Paletz, Gabriel (2001) 'Archives and Archivists Remade: The Paper Print Collection and The Film of Her', *The Moving Image*, 1(1), pp. 68–93.

Pierce, David (2013) *The Survival Rate of American Silent Feature Films 1912-1929*. Washington, DC: Library of Congress. Available at: https://www.loc.gov/programs/static/national-film-preservation-board/documents/pub158.final_version_sept_2013.pdf (accessed on 27 September 2017).

| 151

Punt, Michael (2000) *Early Cinema and the Technological Imaginary.* PhD Dissertation, University of Amsterdam.

Strauven, Wanda (2013) 'Media Archaeology: Where Film History, Media Art, and New Media (Can) Meet', in Julia Noordegraaf, Cosetta Saba, Barbara Le Maitre, and Vinzenz Hediger (eds.) *Preserving and Exhibiting Media Art. Challenges and Perspectives.* Amsterdam: Amsterdam University Press.

Streible, Dan (2009) 'The State of Orphan Films: Editor's Introduction', *The Moving Image, Special Issue on Orphan Film*, 9(1), pp. vi-xix.

Testa, Bart (1992) *Back and Forth: Early Cinema and the Avant-Garde.* Waterloo, Ontario: Wilfrid Laurier University Press.

Walls, Howard (1953) *Motion Pictures 1894-1912. Identified from the Records of the United States Copyright Office.* Washington DC: Library of Congress Copyright Office.

ABOUT THE AUTHOR

Claudy Op den Kamp is Lecturer in Film and faculty member at the Centre for Intellectual Property Policy and Management at Bournemouth University, UK, and Adjunct Research Fellow at Swinburne Law School, Australia.

Conclusion
The Brighton line

Op den Kamp, Claudy, *The Greatest Films Never Seen. The Film Archive and the Copyright Smokescreen*. Amsterdam University Press, 2018

DOI: 10.5117/9789462981393_CONCL

ABSTRACT

The preceding chapters have explored the film archive and the resulting categories of a legal cross section (the embargoed film, the orphan film, and the public domain film), as well as found-footage filmmaking as an artistic practice in which all those categories can be seen to converge. Here, the themes that have emerged in these chapters are drawn together and some thoughts about the overall topic of copyright and digital archival access practices are given – to what extent copyright can be seen as a smokescreen, and to what extent the greatest films are never seen.

KEYWORDS
Brighton line, film archive, copyright smokescreen, greatest films never seen

The Brighton Pier
(CC0)

In this book, we have looked at the various parts of the film archive affected by copyright, focusing in particular on the challenge it represents to digital access. By reshuffling the archive's contents and examining them through the lens of copyright, we discovered a very different story from the one usually told. This new story reveals how copyright ownership, and the tendency to prioritize those films that are legally available, has coloured our understanding of the history of film. Archival film historiography – the way film history is written using archival films, as well as the history of written archival film history itself – is naturally skewed towards those films that are accessible. This book, however, has found a new point of entry into the study of film history; as such, it offers a novel, counterfactual narrative.

THE FILM ARCHIVE

The copyright lens has revealed some important insights into the current state of the film archive, including its historic shift from uncharted territory to a potentially rich primary source for film historians. Even more importantly, it has exposed the way both commercial and not-for-profit archives actively shape access to their holdings and, in doing so, help create a certain version of film history.

This book has taken a specific public-sector film archive (EYE) as a case study in order to explore these insights in greater depth; it first recategorized the archive's holdings, on the basis of copyright ownership, and then subjected the results to a systematic analysis. Its enquiries have necessarily been more empirical than theoretical, but they have demonstrated the conceptual challenges involved in archival access. It illustrated one such challenge by relating the history of a particular film that had been placed under embargo: public archives have a remit both to preserve and to provide access to the film material they hold, but in this particular case, the rights holder had explicitly forbidden the exploitation of the title. After his death, however, the museum's staff successfully negotiated with the rights holder's heirs, and subsequently restored and re-released the film. In this way, it was at last revealed to the world after nearly 40 years of invisibility. Another, differing example was that of an orphan work – that is, a film that was still within the period of copyright but without an identifiable or locatable copyright holder. In this case, after undertaking a risk analysis, EYE took the decision to publish the film on DVD, despite the fact that its rights situation was unclear due to the obscurity of its production company's past. Another archive might well have come to a different decision, and the film would have remained unseen and unacknowledged – representing another lacuna in the history of film. Yet another example was a title that had lapsed into the public domain. This US-produced film was believed lost until it was discovered in the Dutch archive nearly eight decades after its original production date. As the original production and distribution studio had no interest in re-releasing the film, arguably due to its public-domain status, the institute's staff managed to secure the necessary external funding to digitally restore it. These examples from just one archive show how films can remain hidden from public knowledge due to the vagaries of their copyright status; their existence is only revealed to the world if these problems are overcome. Their fate can turn on legal restrictions, chance discoveries, and human decisions.

The book's examination of the artistic intervention made by found-footage filmmaking in the context of this public-sector institution (EYE) has also helped us to investigate further the role of the archive in the creation of a certain film history. The reuse of archival film of course has aesthetic repercussions, but it also foregrounds the fact that the practice of 'doing' history with the films themselves involves (as we saw with the previous examples) the intersection of rights issues, human agency, and the films' potential for history-making. As such, found-footage filmmaking challenges canonical film history and the way that history has been written. The archive itself plays a role in this process: it either acts as an impediment ('gatekeeping') or as a catalyst (providing access to the films in its holdings), revealing the existence of a 'permission culture' inside such institutions. Thus, the film archive and its staff are crucial nodal points in the larger network of actors involved in the debate over archival access.

The archive as a whole is therefore an amalgamation of various facets. This book has dedicated a discrete chapter to an exploration of each of these facets in turn under the heading that best describes this aspect of the archive's role: as terra incognita; as a 'Swiss bank'; as a 'handbag'; as a vehicle of power; and as a birthplace or place of renewal. The new conception of the film archive that has subsequently emerged illustrates that it cannot be envisaged as some sort of future 'celestial multiplex', in which all of its films will be digitally available to all people at all times; rather, it is a go-between, a terminus, or a mediator between the legal restrictions of copyright and the potential of archival films for history-making.

One of the fundamental characteristics of academic research, however, is the need to adopt a critical attitude towards the source material itself – as well as towards its study and use. It goes without saying that this obviously applies to film history. Indeed, ever since the historiographic turn of the late 1970s, the source material of film historians (and the way they use it) has been a topic of intense debate – in particular, the question of the object of study and what should be regarded as evidence. As a result, scholars who engage with filmic sources and other filmic phenomena (which are also subject to broader discussions beyond academia) are called upon to reflect on these sources critically. In order to do so productively, however, it is essential to first contextualize the sources historically, as well as to understand the factors that influence their accessibility, including their legal provenance. However, film studies scholars, and film historians in particular, who use archival films for their research, tend to regard the film archive as simply a place of storage for their primary sources. But this 'storage place' is itself changing in response to digitization and funding pressures. If the field of film studies is to respond appropriately to this rapidly shifting landscape, it is paramount that the field becomes familiar with the inner workings of the film archive, and especially with the practices of archival access.

THE COPYRIGHT SMOKESCREEN

The examination of the Paper Print Collection in the previous chapter has further contributed to our understanding of the historical interaction between film and copyright by revealing the extent to which registration formalities – and their circumvention – helped stabilize the recognition of film as a new medium. In fact, this theme of the complex interaction between the film archive, copyright, and human agency has threaded its way throughout the book as we looked in detail at stories of copyright (and its circumvention) in relation to archival practices and administrative procedures. These stories have shown us how, in order to analyze the potential of archival material to act as historical primary sources, it is essential to take into account the conjunction between the legal context, the material's copyright status, and the human agency behind the 'activation of copyright' involved in these practices.

An examination of the film archive as a safe(guarding) place for potential historical sources reveals that both film history and intellectual property are concepts that are historically and culturally contingent. The book lays no claim to originality in these proposals; however, what is novel is that it has used the idea that intellectual property is a historically and culturally specific concept as the crucial underpinning of its (legal) study into archival access, providing an analytical tool, which can be replicated no matter the context under analysis. It therefore offers a gateway into productive research in other contexts, with the potential to provide fresh insights into such subjects as the relationship between the film industry's dynamics and the shaping of film form. By rethinking the link between the film archive and the potential of its holdings for history-making in relation to the (current and potential) challenges of digitization, the research in this book also resonates beyond the confinement of its specific field to inform broader debates affected by archiving and economics. As such, it is not only relevant to discussions on archival access, but also contributes to the film historiographic debate by opening up questions of particular significance to academics – for example, the consequences for the writing of film history when films are (un)available for legal reasons.

Thus, the idea that archival access is controlled both by those who own the rights and by those who own the physical assets can be extended to other archival contexts. For example, the orphan works problem, often seen as the result of a specific legal discourse, in fact reaches beyond the exclusively legal realm; it is part of the debate over access, irrespective of its archival context – be it a commercial, not-for-profit, national, or regional archive. As we have seen in the practice of EYE, orphan works need not always be problematic. In this respect, it is important to unravel the challenges provoked by the contemporary economics of archival access, while simultaneously recognizing the interplay between the legal aspects of the problem and human agency. Copyright can therefore be used as a sort of 'sieve' through which we can filter the various narratives found in the archive.

In practice, however, 'copyright issues' are too often used instead as a shield to hide behind. Copyright therefore becomes a smokescreen that obscures an infinitely larger issue: the impossibility of providing access to everything that still survives and has been preserved in the archive. In order to understand how we use archival sources to determine what film history is or where (official) film history resides, we have to begin with film history's and film historiography's interconnectedness with the intellectual property system. In this sense, copyright also obscures the very nature of film history itself – that is, the fact that it is a necessarily partial and provisional story, told from the perspective of the present. Any discussions over the potential for future historiography needs to place the public accessibility of source material at the forefront. The orphan works issue, for example, and legal issues more generally, cannot be detached from archival policy decisions, especially if these concern access and distribution. Policies, in turn, must aim to reflect fully the implications of inaccessibility for film history, particularly in the case of unclear ownership. Ideally, they should also include a dialogue with stakeholders, and provide the possibility for historical reinterpretations, even though, at times, these might not be in the interest of some of the stakeholders, whether they be the rights holders or the archive itself.

What happens in practice with orphan works, and what happens outside of the film archival context (particularly in relation to mass digitization), will be paramount when it comes to addressing the legal aspects of these films. So far, the topic of orphan works legislation has been mainly the concern of European institutions in the GLAM sector, predominantly relating to these works' use in educational and noncommercial contexts. It will be important to watch how developments in other contexts in relation to orphan works legislation, such as a commercial context, but also another geographical context (the US, for instance), will pan out in the future.

It is now 40 years since the first substantial collaboration between archivists and historians took place at the FIAF Brighton Congress, an event that raised awareness of the issues involved in the availability and the unavailability of source material. However, control in a 'post-scarcity' world presents a different dilemma, especially where the relationship between the archivist and the historian is potentially diluted as researchers make fewer physical visits to international archives, conducting their research online, limited by what is digitized. However, scholars will continue to rely on archives and archivists to provide them with their research material—the presence of the human gatekeeper despite the digital form of the archive—and the negotiation between them has to be based on transparency, not occluded by a copyright smokescreen.

THE GREATEST FILMS NEVER SEEN

Reshuffling the film archive has exposed the fact that parts of archival collections are not publicly accessible. The discovery of one 'orphaned' collection always seems to unveil yet another, unavailable one, and it appears that the fragmentary state of the archive cannot be resolved.

The stories in this book have only skimmed the surface of this dilemma. Undoubtedly, there are countless other, untold stories that we could unearth to illustrate the dichotomy between the intellectual and material ownership of archival source material, and the effect this has on the writing of film history. But the most important point to take away from all of this relates to the agency of the archivists – a neglected component in the debates on archival access. Indeed, it appears to matter a great deal whether the archivist tries to exercise agency in a national archive or a regional one, or even outside the institutional context altogether. Furthermore, of course, it also matters whether they are trying to do so in a nonprofit context or in a more commercial one.

In this respect, EYE is, in some senses, unique: the institution is situated at the intersection of the two dichotomies that underpin the discussion in this book – the difference between canonical textbook film histories and the actual material holdings of a film archive, and the difference between intellectual and material property. Moreover, the composition of its collection, its public mission, and its (specifically Dutch) pragmatism go hand in hand. Its public mission to provide access to its holdings, combined with its large quantity of marginal and noncanonical film material and the way it has made its own collection the central focus of its access and presentation activities, means that EYE has been able (or has chosen) to respond to historiographical shifts and artistic interventions. The composition of the collection and its focus on the specific aesthetic qualities of its archival film material has led the institute to develop new archival policies. As such, it has been instrumental in the development and revision of written film history, based on what it has made available throughout the last few decades.

However, EYE's pragmatic 'can-do' attitude and the agency exercised by its staff might be particular to the Dutch (legal) situation, and cannot be considered separately from the organizational, social, and political climate it inhabits. A significant element contributing to the institute's attitude is the fact that its risk analyses have been made in the knowledge that (to date) no rights holders have ever come forward after it has made a work public without permission. Again, this attitude is no doubt reinforced by the fact that EYE holds the kind of collection that allows for such risks and the institute itself is situated in a country that is averse to litigation, meaning that it is not dominated by the culture of fear that prevails elsewhere, and where a wrong is not as 'potentially punitive' (Aufderheide and Jaszi, 2011, p. 148) as, for instance, in the United States. It is therefore no surprise that the legal scholar P. Bernt Hugenholtz (cited in Aufderheide and Jaszi, 2011), who professes that you should not fear copyright, is Dutch.

Although this book has looked at certain aspects that could be considered unique to the Netherlands, some of its findings can be extended to other contexts. Copyright is an important filter to add to the list of historical and contemporary factors that influence what material is potentially available and publicly accessible. A clear copyright ownership situation fosters film restoration projects: sometimes this means that the ownership of the material is undisputed and a large sum of money can then be invested in its preservation and access; sometimes it means that the film survives as unique material that is in the public domain. Whatever the context, copyright should, indeed, not be feared. If a heritage institution is properly informed about the nature of copyright, including the differences in international legal interpretations, it will not have to be excessively cautious (although 'ethical' obligations will remain); it will, rather, be able to ensure a confident access policy that will expand the range of possibilities of what can be done with the material.

The book has focused on a somewhat historical analysis, taking a retrospective consideration of film and the potential reverberations for film historiography. However, as a reflective academic practice, it could also provide a starting point for a consideration of comparable phenomena in a more general contemporary media landscape, particularly an analysis of media consumption practices, and could therefore be beneficial for others who investigate similar questions in different spheres of the media.

The study has not been centred on a specific methodology; rather, it has used a specific perspective – the filter of copyright ownership – to examine the practice of film archival access. The analysis can therefore be extended in several directions. Obvious examples would be related to practices that are already embedded in a legal discourse, such as file-sharing or peer-to-peer networks. As opposed to concentrating on the binary opposition of 'legal' versus 'illegal', or the detrimental effects these networks arguably have on the music or film industry (Patry, 2009; Johns, 2010), it might be more meaningful to recast such networks as mediators between the owners and users of copyrighted material. This would enable their analysis in a wider historically, geographically, socially, technologically, and legally contingent context.

Other areas of practice with immediate political as well as cultural dimensions (which potentially impede access to and exploitation of the work) could equally benefit from being freed from the confines of an exclusively legal debate. One such example is academic publishing in the digital realm, in which problems relating to the protection, accessibility, and exploitation of material are currently amplified by issues of digital technology and human agency.

Perhaps this book's most significant contribution is the way it re-situates the discussion of archival access by proposing that it is the role of legality, combined with the activity of human agents, that governs archival material's potential for history-making. Placing the historical narrative in the frame of intellectual property – and copyright specifically – adds an essential but previously unrealized dimension to the debate.

By way of conclusion, then, let us return one last time to baby Jack, whom we met at the very outset of our narrative exploration. Jack's journey took him from a child with an equivocal social status to a grown man who has been fully accepted into high society. Our orphan film took an equivalent journey, starting out as a problematic title located in an institutional setting and finishing as a phenomenon that is, under certain circumstances, subject to legal recognition on an EU level. Both Jack and the orphan film have arrived at the terminus and now face a potentially prosperous future.

The significance of the Brighton line in Wilde's play is that the provenance of baby Jack signaled that he had belonged in high society all along; he was just displaced from his proper role in life for a while. The orphan film, however, might have gained a certain legality but its acceptance into the larger historical narrative still appears to be quite uncertain, based on, amongst other things, its provenance. As stated in the Introduction, the line is *everything*. Current exceptions for use only apply to its educational and noncommercial uses in the GLAM sector. Its journey has not yet ended and there still seems to be some way to go.

Jack ends up with his intended, Gwendolen, just as Theodora Fitzgerald ends up with Rudolph Valentino in the final scene. Our orphan film has similarly ended up with the Orphan Works Directive. But only time will tell how their stories will develop in the future. We hope for the best for them, but their lives after the final credits will doubtless not be entirely happy-ever-after. For a final thought, we might need to look to one of the other characters in *The Importance of Being Earnest*, Algernon Moncrieff, who turns out to be Jack's brother. Algernon claims: 'I really don't see anything romantic in proposing. It is very romantic to be in love. But there is nothing romantic about a definite proposal. Why, one may be accepted. One usually is, I believe. Then the excitement is all over. The very essence of romance is uncertainty.'

It may be that a little uncertainty is the very opening we need. The world outside the archive is changing drastically fast, and, as we have seen throughout the themes explored in this book, certain practices outside of the institutional context of the archive, in which filmmakers have ready access to the necessary material, have put and are putting the very concept of the archive under pressure. So, whether the classic gatekeepers will be able to 'let go' of their collections, acknowledging the new role of users, while their 'institutional need to control risk may impinge on our rights as users' (Aufderheide and Jaszi, 2011, p. 8) remains to be seen. Pat Aufderheide and Peter Jaszi (2011, p. 5) fabulously state that the 'key to challenging the culture of fear and doubt is knowledge. Knowledge unlocks the door to action, which lets you join the culture of creativity', which can lead to a true balance between ownership and exchange of ideas. It is that knowledge that can enable us to leave room for uncertainty – the uncertainty of untold and unexpected stories yet to unfold.

BIBLIOGRAPHY

Aufderheide, Patricia and Peter Jaszi (2011) *Reclaiming Fair Use. How to Put Balance Back in Copyright*. Chicago: The University of Chicago Press.

Johns, Adrian (2010) *Piracy. The Intellectual Property Wars From Gutenberg to Gates*. Chicago: University of Chicago Press.

Patry, William (2009) *Moral Panics and the Copyright Wars*. New York: Oxford University Press.

ABOUT THE AUTHOR

Claudy Op den Kamp is Lecturer in Film and faculty member at the Centre for Intellectual Property Policy and Management at Bournemouth University, UK, and Adjunct Research Fellow at Swinburne Law School, Australia.

FILMOGRAPHY

À BOUT DE SOUFFLE ('BREATHLESS', FR 1960, Jean-Luc Godard)
ALS TWEE DRUPPELS WATER ('LIKE TWO DROPS OF WATER', NL 1963, Fons Rademakers)
BEYOND THE ROCKS (US 1922, Sam Wood)
BITS & PIECES (NL 1990 - present, EYE)
CASABLANCA (US 1942, Michael Curtiz)
CHARADE (US 1963, Stanley Donen)
CITIZEN KANE (US 1941, Orson Welles)
DE OVERVAL ('THE SILENT RAID', NL 1962, Paul Rotha)
DOWNHILL (UK 1927, Alfred Hitchcock)
DUCK AND COVER (US 1951, Anthony Rizzo)
EDISON KINETOSCOPIC RECORD OF A SNEEZE (US 1894, Thomas Edison)
FANFARE (NL 1958, Bert Haanstra)
FILM IST. 1-6, 7-12 (AT 1998, 2002, Gustav Deutsch)
FILM IST. A GIRL & A GUN (AT 2009, Gustav Deutsch)
GRAVITY (BE 2007, Nicolas Provost)
HOME STORIES (GE 1990, Matthias Müller)
HUGO (US 2011, Martin Scorcese)
IL GATTOPARDO ('The Leopard', IT 1963, Luchino Visconti)
JULES ET JIM (FR 1962, Francois Truffaut)
LOS ANGELES PLAYS ITSELF (US 2003, Thom Andersen)
LYRISCH NITRAAT ('LYRICAL NITRATE', NL 1991, Peter Delpeut)
MAUDITE SOIT LA GUERRE ('WAR IS HELL', BE 1914, Alfred Machin)
MENSEN VAN MORGEN ('PEOPLE OF TOMORROW', NL 1964, Kees Brusse)
NANOOK OF THE NORTH (US 1922, Robert Flaherty)
OTTO E MEZZO ($8\frac{1}{2}$, IT 1963, Federico Fellini)
TAXI DRIVER (US 1976, Martin Scorsese)
THE ASPHALT JUNGLE (US 1950, John Huston)

THE BRIDGE ON THE RIVER KWAI (US 1957, David Lean)
THE CLOCK (UK 2010, Christian Marclay)
THE GREAT TRAIN ROBBERY (US 1903, Edwin S. Porter)
THE SOUND OF THE END OF MUSIC (UK 2010, Vicky Bennett)
WARFARE OF THE FLESH (US 1917, Edward Warren)

BIBLIOGRAPHY

A Matter of Rights: A Talk with Lee Tsiantis (2010) Available at: http://selfstyledsiren.
blogspot.ch/2010/02/matter-of-rights-talk-with-lee-tsiantis.html (accessed on 21 April 2016).

Association of European Cinémathèques (ACE) (2010) *Results of the Survey on Orphan Works 2009/10*. Brussels: ACE. Available at: http://www.ace-film.eu/wp-content/ uploads/2011/12/ACE_Orphan_Works_Survey_Results_final_1004014.pdf (accessed on 11 October 2017).

Alberdingk Thijm, Christiaan (2008) *Waarom je beter geen regisseur kunt worden. Tips over auteursrecht en contracten voor als je het toch bent*. Amsterdam: Dutch Directors Guild.

Allen, Barry ([retired] Executive Director of Broadcast Services and Film Preservation, Paramount Pictures) (2010) Interviewed by Claudy Op den Kamp. Philadelphia, US, 4 November.

Allen, Robert, and Douglas Gomery (1985) *Film History. Theory and Practice*. New York: McGraw-Hill.

Amad, Paula (2010) *Counter-Archive. Film, the Everyday, and Albert Kahn's Archives de la Planète*. New York: Columbia University Press.

Andersen, Thom (2010) 'At the Digital Intersection', *Reimagining the Archive: Remapping and Remixing Traditional Models in the Digital Age*, University of California Los Angeles, Los Angeles, 12–14 November.

Anderson, Steve (2011) *Technologies of History: Visual Media and the Eccentricity of the Past*. Hanover: Dartmouth College Press.

Angelopoulos, Christina (2012) 'Determining the Term of Protection for Films: When Does a Film Fall into the Public Domain in Europe?', *IRIS Plus*, 2, pp. 7-21.

Arnold, John (2000) *History. A Very Short Introduction*. Oxford: Oxford University Press.

Aufderheide, Patricia and Peter Jaszi (2004) *Untold Stories: Creative Consequences of the Rights Clearance Culture for Documentary Filmmakers*. Washington, DC: Center for Social Media, American University.

Aufderheide, Patricia and Peter Jaszi (2011) *Reclaiming Fair Use. How to Put Balance Back in Copyright*. Chicago: The University of Chicago Press.

Bandura, Albert (2006) 'Toward a Psychology of Human Agency', *Perspectives on Psychological Science*, 1(2), pp. 164–180. Available at: http://journals.sagepub.com/doi/abs/10.1111/j.1745-6916.2006.00011.x (accessed on 16 October 2017).

Barnes, Mike (2015) '"Ghostbusters", "Top Gun", "Shawshank" Enter National Film Registry', *Hollywood Reporter*, 16 December [Online]. Available at: http://www.hollywoodreporter.com/news/ghostbusters-top-gun-enter-national-849092 (accessed on 22 January 2016)

Barten, Egbert (2002) 'Een verloren klassieker', *Skrien*, 34(8), pp. 22–24.

Bently, Lionel, and Brad Sherman (2014) *Intellectual Property Law*. 4th ed. Oxford: Oxford University Press.

Beerekamp, Hans (2002) 'Wie kent de film van Freddy?', *NRC Handelsblad*, 4 January 2002.

Bellido, José (2014) 'Howe and Griffiths' Concepts of Property in Intellectual Property', *Birkbeck Law Review*, 2(1), pp. 147–156.

Bertoni, Aura, Flavia Guerrieri, and Maria Lillà Montagnani (2017) *Report 2. Requirements for Diligent Search in 20 European Countries*. Bournemouth: EnDOW. Available at: http://diligentsearch.eu/wp-content/uploads/2017/06/REPORT-2.pdf (accessed on 11 October 2017).

Blakely, Megan, Kerry Patterson, Victoria Stobo, Simon Tanner, and Andrea Wallace (2017) *Copyright and Cultural Memory: Digital Conference Proceedings*. Glasgow: CREATe. Available at: http://ccm.create.ac.uk/ (accessed on 11 October 2017).

Borde, Raymond (1983) *Les Cinémathèques*. Lausanne: Editions L'Age d'Homme.

Bordwell, David (1997) *On the History of Film Style*. Cambridge: Harvard University Press.

Bordwell, David (2013) 'A Celestial Cinémathèque? or, Film Archives and Me: A Semi-Personal History', in Cinémathèque royale de Belgique (ed.) *75000 Films*. Crisnée: Editions Yellow Now, pp. 67–82.

Bordwell, David, and Kristin Thompson (1994) *Film History. An Introduction*. New York: McGraw-Hill.

Borghi, Maurizio, and Stavroula Karapapa (2013) *Copyright and Mass Digitization. A Cross-Jurisdictional Perspective*. Oxford: Oxford University Press.

Borghi, Maurizio, Kris Erickson, and Marcella Favale (2016) 'With Enough Eyeballs All Searches Are Diligent: Mobilizing the Crowd in Copyright Clearance for Mass Digitization', *Chicago-Kent Journal of Intellectual Property*, 16(1), pp. 135–166.

Bout, Leontien (2017) 'Dealing with Orphan Works, a Dutch Film Archive's Perspective', EnDOW publication. Available at: http://diligentsearch.eu/wp-content/uploads/2017/11/L-Bout-presentation-orphan-works-a-film-archives-perspective.pdf (accessed on 9 November 2017).

Bowser, Eileen (1979) 'The Brighton Project: An Introduction', *Quarterly Review of Film Studies*, pp. 509–538.

Boyle, James (2003) 'The Second Enclosure Movement and the Construction of the Public Domain', *Law and Contemporary Problems*, 66, pp. 33–74.

Boyle, James (2008) *The Public Domain: Enclosing the Commons of the Mind*. New Haven: Yale University Press.

Bracht, Maarten van (2012) 'Freddy's motieven' [Online]. Available at: http://boeken. vpro.nl/artikelen/2012/oktober/de-donkere-kamer-van-damokles.html (accessed on 27 April 2014).

Brainin-Donnenberg, Wilbrig, and Michael Loebenstein (eds.) (2009) *Gustav Deutsch*. Vienna: Filmmuseum Synema Publikationen.

Brown, Richard (1996) 'The British Film Copyright Archive', in Colin Harding and Simon Popple (eds.) *In the Kingdom of Shadows: Companion to Early Cinema*. London: Cygnus Arts, pp. 240–245.

Buccafusco, Chris, and Paul Heald (2013) 'Do Bad Things Happen When Works Fall into the Public Domain? Empirical Tests of Copyright Term Extension', *Berkeley Tech. L.J.*, 28(1), pp. 1–43.

Cave, Richard Allen (ed.) (2000) *The Importance of Being Earnest, and Other Plays*. London: Penguin Classics.

Chapman, James, Mark Glancy, and Sue Harper (eds.) (2007) *The New Film History. Sources, Methods, Approaches*. Basingstoke: Palgrave Macmillan.

Cherchi Usai, Paolo (1996) 'The Early Years. Origins and Survival', in Geoffrey Nowell-Smith (ed.) *The Oxford History of World Cinema*. Oxford: Oxford University Press, pp. 6-12.

Cherchi Usai, Paolo (2000) *Silent Cinema: An Introduction*. London: British Film Institute.

Cherchi Usai, Paolo (2009) 'Are All (Analog) Films "Orphans"? A Pre-digital Appraisal', *The Moving Image*, 9(1), pp. 1–18.

Christensen, Thomas (2010) 'Film Archive Preservation Strategies', *Archiving the Future conference*, University of York, 28 February.

Christensen, Thomas (2017) 'How to Destroy Film Heritage', *fi:re Film Restoration Summit*, Polish Film Institute, 9-10 November.

Christie, Ian (2013) 'New Lamps for Old: What Can we Expect From Archival Film Festivals?', in Alex Marlow-Mann (ed.) *Film Festival Yearbook 5: Archival Film Festivals*. St. Andrews: St. Andrews Film Studies, pp. 41–53.

Codell, Julie (2010) '"Second Hand Images": On Art's Surrogate Means and Media-Introduction', *Visual Resources*, 26(3), pp. 214-215.

Daly, Angela (2016) *Socio-Legal Aspects of the 3D Printing Revolution*. London: Palgrave-MacMillan.

David, Matthew, and Debora Halbert (eds.) (2014) *The SAGE Handbook of Intellectual Property*. London: SAGE Publications Ltd.

De Klerk, Nico (2009) 'Designing a Home; Orphan Films in the Work of Gustav Deutsch', in Wilbrig Brainin-Donnenberg and Michael Loebenstein (eds.) *Gustav Deutsch*. Vienna: Filmmuseum Synema Publikationen, pp. 113-122.

Deazley, Ronan (2006) *Rethinking Copyright: History, Theory, Language*. Northampton: Edward Elgar.

Deazley, Ronan (2017) 'Copyright 101', *Copyright Cortex* [online] available at: https://copyrightcortex.org/copyright-101 (accessed on 25 September 2017).

Decherney, Peter (2012) *Hollywood Copyright Wars*. New York: Columbia University Press.

de Kuyper, Eric (1991) 'Een averechtse filmgeschiedenis I; Fragmenten', *Versus*, (1), pp. 7-16.

de Kuyper, Eric (1994) 'Anyone for an Aesthetics of Film History?', *Film History*, 6(1), pp. 100-109.

de Kuyper, Eric (2013) 'Werken bij een Filmarchief/Filmmuseum, of: Schizofrenie als opdracht', in Cinemathèque royale de Belgique (ed.) *75000 Films*. Crisnée: Editions Yellow Now, pp. 121-137.

Delpeut, Peter (1990) 'BITS & PIECES - De grenzen van het filmarchief', *Versus*, 2, pp. 75-84.

Delpeut, Peter (1997) *Cinéma Perdu. De eerste dertig jaar van de film 1895-1925*. Amsterdam: Uitgeverij Bas Lubberhuizen.

Delpeut, Peter (1998) *Juryrapport Sphinx Cultuurprijs 1998*. Maastricht: N.V. Koninklijke Sphinx Gustavsberg, pp. 1-5.

Delpeut, Peter (2012) 'An Unexpected Reception. LYRICAL NITRATE Between Film History and Art', in Marente Bloemheuvel, Giovanna Fossati, and Jaap Guldemond (eds.) *Found Footage. Cinema Exposed*. Amsterdam: Amsterdam University Press/EYE Film Institute Netherlands, pp. 218-224.

Delpeut, Peter (2018) 'Prologue. Questions of Colours: Taking Sides', in Giovanna Fossati, Victoria Jackson, Bregt Lameris, Elif Rongen, Sarah Street, and Joshua Yumibe (eds.) *The Colour Fantastic. Chromatic Worlds of Silent Cinema*. Amsterdam: Amsterdam University Press.

Derclaye, Estelle (ed.) (2009) *BILETA conference*. The University of Winchester Law School, 30 March [Online]. Available at: http://works.bepress.com/cgi/viewcontent.cgi?article=1023&context=estelle_derclaye (accessed on 21 April 2016).

Derclaye, Estelle (ed.) (2010) *Copyright and Cultural Heritage. Preservation and Access to Works in a Digital World*. Cheltenham: Edward Elgar Publishing.

Dessem, Matthew (2006) '#57: CHARADE', *The Criterion Contraption*, 2 July. [Online]. Available at: http://criterioncollection.blogspot.com/2006_07_01_archive.html (accessed on 21 April 2016).

Deutsch, Gustav (2010) Interviewed by Claudy Op den Kamp. Gorizia, IT, 22 March.

Deutsch, Gustav (2010) Interviewed by Claudy Op den Kamp. New York, US, 10 April.

Donaldson, Michael (2014) *Clearance & Copyright. Everything You Need to Know for Film and Television*. 4th ed. West Hollywood. Silman-James Press.

Doros, Dennis (Vice President, Milestone Film & Video) (2010) Interviewed by Claudy Op den Kamp, Philadelphia, US, 5 November.

Duke Center for the Study of the Public Domain (2005) *Access to Orphan Works*. [Online]. Available at: http://web.law.duke.edu/cspd/pdf/cspdorphanfilm.pdf (accessed on 21 April 2016).

Dupin, Christophe (2013) 'First Tango in Paris: The Birth of FIAF, 1936-1938', *The Journal of Film Preservation*, 88, pp. 43-57.

Dusollier, Séverine (2010) *Scoping Study on Copyright and Related Rights and the Public Domain*. Namur: WIPO.

Edgerton, Gary (2000) 'The Germans Wore Gray, You Wore Blue: Frank Capra, Casablanca, and the Colorization Controversy of the 1980s', *Journal of Popular Film and Television,* 27(4), pp. 24-32.

Edison, Thomas (1894) 'Edison's Invention of the Kineto-Phonograph', *The Century, A Popular Quarterly*, 48(2), pp. 206-214.

Elferink, Mirjam and Allard Ringnalda (2008) *Digitale Ontsluiting van Historische Archieven en Verweesde Werken: Een Inventarisatie*. Utrecht: CIER [Online]. Available at: http://www.wodc.nl/onderzoeksdatabase/ontsluiting-historische-archieven-en-auteursrecht-hoe-beter.aspx?cp=44&cs=6796 (accessed on 21 April 2016).

Elsaesser, Thomas (1986) 'The New Film History', *Sight & Sound*, 55(4), pp. 246–251.

Elsaesser, Thomas (ed.) (1990) *Early Cinema. Space, Frame, Narrative*. London: British Film Institute.

Enticknap, Leo (2007) 'Have Digital Technologies Reopened the Lindgren/Langlois Debate?', *Spectator*, 27(1), pp. 10–20.

European Film Gateway (EFG) (2009) *Report on legal frameworks in European Film Gateway (EFG) consortium member states*. Amsterdam: European Film Gateway [Online]. Available at: http://www.edfgproject.eu/downloads/D.5.1_legal_frameworks_in_EFG_consortium_a.pdf (accessed on 21 April 2016).

European Film Gateway (EFG) (2010) *Final Guidelines on Copyright Clearance and IPR Management*. Amsterdam: European Film Gateway [Online]. Available at: pro.europeana.eu/documents/.../EFG_D5.3_Copyright_Clearance.pdf (accessed on 4 November 2010).

Favale, Marcella, Fabian Homberg, Martin Kretschmer, Dinusha Mendis, and Davide Secchi (2013) *Copyright, and the Regulation of Orphan Works: A comparative review of seven jurisdictions and a rights clearance simulation*. CREATe working paper. Available at: http://www.create.ac.uk/publications/copyright-and-the-regulation-of-orphan-works/ (accessed on 11 October 2017).

Favale, Marcella, Simone Schroff, and Aura Bertoni (2016) *Report 1. Requirements for Diligent Search in the United Kingdom, the Netherlands, and Italy*. Bournemouth: EnDOW. Available at: http://diligentsearch.eu/wp-content/uploads/2016/05/EnDOW_Report-1.pdf (accessed on 11 October 2017).

Feltenstein, George (2010) 'New Platforms', *Re-imagining the Archive. Remapping and Remixing Traditional Models in the Digital Era*, University of California Los Angeles, 10-12 November 2010.

Fernandez Escareño, Itzia (2009) *La Compilation. Un Outil Paradoxal de Valorisation des Films Muets Recyclés par Peter Delpeut et Coproduits par le Nederlands Filmmuseum (1989-1999)*. PhD Dissertation. Université Sorbonne Nouvelle – Paris 3.

Finler, Joel (2003) *The Hollywood Story*. London and New York: Wallflower Press.

First Person: Restoring Film with Digital Recombination (2012) Available at: http://www.creativeplanetnetwork.com/news/news-articles/first-person-restoring-film-digital-recombination/370596 (accessed on 21 April 2016).

Fishman, Stephen (2017) *The Public Domain. How to Find and Use Copyright-Free Writings, Music, Art and More*. 8th ed., Berkeley: NOLO.

Fossati, Giovanna (2009) *From Grain to Pixel: The Archival Life of Film in Transition*. Amsterdam: Amsterdam University Press.

Fossati, Giovanna (2012) 'Found Footage. Filmmaking, Film Archiving and New Participatory Platforms', in Marente Bloemheuvel, Giovanna Fossati, and Jaap Guldemond (eds.) *Found Footage. Cinema Exposed*. Amsterdam: Amsterdam University Press/EYE Film Institute Netherlands, pp. 177–184.

Fossati, Giovanna, and Nanna Verhoeff (2007) 'Beyond Distribution: Some Thoughts on the Future of Archival Films', in Frank Kessler and Nanna Verhoeff (eds.) *Networks of Entertainment: Early Film Distribution 1895-1915*. Eastleigh: John Libbey, pp. 331–339.

Fossati, Giovanna, Victoria Jackson, Bregt Lameris, Elif Rongen, Sarah Street, and Joshua Yumibe (eds.) (2018) *The Colour Fantastic. Chromatic Worlds of Silent Cinema*. Amsterdam: Amsterdam University Press.

Foucault, Michel (1972) *The Archaeology of Knowledge and the Discourse on Language*. Translated by Alan Mark Sheridan-Smith. New York: Pantheon Books.

Foucault, Michel (1978) *The History of Sexuality, Volume I: An Introduction*. Translated by Robert Hurley. New York: Random House, Inc.

Frick, Caroline (2011) *Saving Cinema. The Politics of Preservation*. New York: Oxford University Press.

Friend, Tad (2016) 'The Mogul of the Middle', *The New Yorker* [Online] Available at: http://www.newyorker.com/magazine/2016/01/11/the-mogul-of-the-middle.

Gaddis, John Lewis (2002) *The Landscape of History. How Historians Map the Past*. Oxford: Oxford University Press.

Gaudreault, André (ed.) (1982) *Cinema 1900-1906. Part 2: Filmography*. Brussels: International Federation of Film Archives (FIAF).

Gauthier, Philippe (2011) 'L'histoire amateur et l'histoire universitaire: paradigmes de l'historiographie du cinéma', *Cinémas: revue d'études cinématographiques*, 21(2-3), pp. 87–105.

Gartenberg, John (1984) 'The Brighton Project: Archives and Historians', *IRIS*, 2(1), pp. 5–16.

Geller, Paul (2016) 'International Copyright: The Introduction', in Lionel Bently (ed.) *International Copyright Law and Practice*. LexisNexis. Available online at: http://www.internationalcopyrightguide.com (accessed on 29 October 2017).

Gomery, Douglas (1985 [1976]) 'Writing the History of the American Film Industry: Warner Brothers and Sound', in Bill Nichols (ed.) *Movies and Methods: An Anthology. Volume II*. Berkeley and Los Angeles: University of California Press, pp. 109–120.

Gorini, Sabina (2004) 'The Protection of Cinematographic Heritage in Europe', *IRIS Plus, a supplement to IRIS, Legal Observations of the European Audiovisual Observatory*, 08, pp. 1–8.

Gowers, Andrew (2006) *Gowers Review of Intellectual Property*. HM Treasury.

Grainge, Paul (1999) 'Reclaiming Heritage: Colourization, Culture Wars and the Politics of Nostalgia', *Cultural Studies*, 13(4), pp. 621–638.

Grainge, Paul, Mark Jancovich, and Sharon Monteith (eds.) (2007) *Film Histories. An Introduction and Reader*. Toronto and Buffalo: University of Toronto Press.

Grimm, Charles (1999) 'A Paper Print Pre-History', *Film History*, 11(2), pp. 204–216.

Grunberg, Arnon (2013) *Buster Keaton lacht nooit*. Amsterdam: Nijgh & Van Ditmar.

Gunning, Tom (1990) 'The Cinema of Attraction: Early Film, Its Spectator and the Avant-Garde', in Thomas Elsaesser (ed.) *Early Cinema. Space, Frame, Narrative*. London: British Film Institute, pp. 229–235.

Habib, André (2006) 'Ruin, Archive and the time of Cinema: Peter Delpeut's LYRICAL NITRATE', *SubStance* #110, 35(2), pp. 120–139.

Habib, André (2007a) 'Le temps décomposé: ruines et cinéma', Protée, 35(2), pp. 15–26.

Habib, André (2007b) 'Des fragments des premiers temps à l'esthétique de la ruine', in Frank Kessler and Nanna Verhoeff (eds.) *Networks of Entertainment: Early Film Distribution 1895-1915*. Eastleigh: John Libbey, pp. 320-326.

Hargreaves, Ian (2011) *The Hargreaves Review of Intellectual Property and Growth*. Independent report [Online]. Available at: http://www.ipo.gov.uk/ipreview-final-report.pdf (accessed on 21 April 2016).

Hausheer, Cecilia, and Christoph Settle (1992) (eds.) *Found Footage Film*. Luzern: Viper/Zyklop Verlag.

Heald, Paul (2014) 'How Copyright Keeps Works Disappeared', *Empirical Legal Studies*, 11(4), pp. 829–866.

Heaney, Stuart (Rights and Contracts Officer Mediathèque and Screen Online, British Film Institute) (2010) Interviewed by Claudy Op den Kamp, London, UK, 26 October.

Hediger, Vinzenz (2005) 'The Original is Always Lost', in Marijke de Valck and Malte Hagener (eds.) *Cinephilia. Movies, Love and Memory*. Amsterdam: Amsterdam University Press.

| 173

Heller, Franziska, and Barbara Flueckiger (2017) Digitale Langzeitsicherung: Nachhaltige Verfügbarkeit und Verwertbarkeit von (digitalen) Filmen – Praxen, Erfahrungen, Probleme. Deliverable in the DIASTOR research project. Available at: https://diastor.ch/digitale-langzeitsicherung/ (accessed on 9 October 2017).

Hendriks, Annemieke (1996) *Huis van illusies. De geschiedenis van paviljoen Vondelpark en het Nederlands Filmmuseum*. Amsterdam: Bas Lubberhuizen.

Hertogs, Daan, and Nico de Klerk (eds.) (1994) *Nonfiction from the Teens. The 1994 Amsterdam Workshop*. Amsterdam: Stichting Nederlands Filmmuseum.

Hertogs, Daan, and Nico de Klerk (eds.) (1996) *Disorderly Order: Colours in Silent Film. The 1995 Amsterdam Workshop*. Amsterdam: Stichting Nederlands Filmmuseum.

High Level Expert Group (HLG; i2010: Digital Libraries) (2008) *Report on Digital Preservation, Orphan Works, and Out-of-Print Works*. [Online]. Available at: http://ec.europa.eu/information_society/activities/digital_libraries/doc/hleg/reports/copyright/copyright_subgroup_final_report_26508-clean171.pdf (accessed on 21 April 2016).

Hilderbrand, Lucas (2009) *Inherent Vice: Bootleg Histories of Videotape and Copyright*. Durham: Duke University Press.

Holman, Roger (ed.) (1982) *Cinema 1900-1906. Part 1: An Analytical Study by the National Film Archive (London) and the International Federation of Film Archives*. Brussels: International Federation of Film Archives (FIAF).

Horak, Jan-Christopher (2007) 'The Gap Between 1 and 0: Digital Video and the Omissions of Film History', *Spectator*, 27(1), pp. 29–41.

Horak, Jan-Christopher, Alain Lacasse, and Paolo Cherchi Usai (1991) 'FIAF Conference, Lisbon, 1989: The Brighton FIAF Conference (1978): Ten Years After', *Historical Journal of Film, Radio & Television,* 11(3), pp. 279–292.

Horwatt, Eli (2009) 'A Taxonomy of Digital Video Remixing: Contemporary Found Footage Practice on the Internet', in Iain Smith (ed.) *Cultural Borrowings. Appropriation, Reworking, Transformation*. Nottingham: Scope: An Online Journal of Film and Television Studies, pp. 76-91.

Houston, Penelope (1994) *Keepers of the Frame: The Film Archives*. London: British Film Institute.

Hoyt, Eric (2011) 'The Future of Selling the Past; Studio Libraries in the 21st Century', *ejumpcut*, [Online]. Available at: http://www.ejumpcut.org/archive/jc52.2010/hoytStudioLibraries/ (accessed on 21 April 2016).

Hudson, Emily, and Andrew Kenyon (2007) 'Digital Access: The Impact of Copyright in Digitisation Practices in Australian Museums, Galleries, Libraries and Archives', *UNSW Law Journal*, 30(1), pp. 12–52.

Hunter, Dan (2012) *The Oxford Introductions to U.S. Law: Intellectual Property*. New York: Oxford University Press.

Hunter, Dan (2017) 'Blockchains, Orphan Works and the Public Domain', *New Approaches to the Orphan Works Problem* [conference], Bournemouth University, 23 June.

Hugenholtz, Bernt, Antoon Quaedvlieg, and Dirk Visser (eds.) (2012) *A Century of Dutch Copyright Law: Auteurswet 1912–2012.* Amsterdam: deLex.

In memoriam Hoos Blotkamp (2014) [Online]. Available at: http://www.programma.eyefilm.nl/nieuws/in-memoriam-hoos-blotkamp (accessed on 19 October 2014).

Intellectual Property Office (IPO) (2014) *Orphan Works Diligent Search Guidance for Applicants: Film and Sound.* Newport: Intellectual Property Office.

Instituut voor Informatierecht (IViR) (2006) *The Recasting of Copyright & Related Rights for the Knowledge Economy.* [Online]. Available at: http://ec.europa.eu/internal_market/copyright/docs/studies/etd2005imd195recast_report_2006.pdf (accessed on 21 April 2016).

JISC (2009) *In From the Cold: An Assessment of the Scope of 'Orphan Works' and Its Impact on the Delivery of Services to the Public.* Strategic Content Alliance, Collections Trust [Online]. Available at: http://www.jisc.ac.uk/publications/reports/2009/infromthecold.aspx (accessed on 21 April 2016).

Johns, Adrian (2010) *Piracy. The Intellectual Property Wars From Gutenberg to Gates.* Chicago: University of Chicago Press.

Jones, Janna (2012) *The Past is a Moving Picture. Preserving the Twentieth Century on Film.* Gainesville: University Press of Florida.

Kamina, Pascal (2016) *Film Copyright in the European Union.* Cambridge: Cambridge University Press.

Keathley, Christian (2006) *Cinephilia and History, or the Wind in the Trees.* Bloomington: Indiana University Press.

Kirste, Lynne (Special Collections Curator, Academy Film Archive) (2010) Interviewed by Claudy Op den Kamp, Los Angeles, US, 15 November.

Klawans, Stuart (1990) 'Rose-Tinted Spectacles', in Mark Crispin Miller (ed.) *Seeing Through Movies.* New York: Pantheon Books, pp. 150–185.

Klimpel, Paul (ed.) (2011) *Bewegte Bilder—Starres Recht? Das Filmerbe und seine rechtlichen Rahmenbedingungen.* Berlin: Berlin Academic.

Koerber, Martin (2008) 'Why Restoration Does not Change Copyright', 64th International Federation of Film Archives (FIAF) Congress, Paris, 17-26 April.

Kohs, David (1988) 'Paint Your Wagon-Please!: Colorization, Copyright, and the Search for Moral Rights', *Federal Communications Law Journal*, 40, pp. 1–38.

Kuhn, Annette, and Jackie Stacey (1998) (eds.) *Screen Histories. A Screen Reader.* Oxford: Clarendon Press.

Kuiper, John, Jacques Ledoux, and others (1975) 'Transcript of Discussion', *Cinema Journal*, 14(2), special edition 'Symposium on the Methodology of Film History', pp. 46–63.

Lameris, Bregt (2007) *Opnieuw belicht: de pas de deux tussen de filmmuseale praktijk en filmhistorische debatten.* PhD Dissertation, Universiteit Utrecht.

Lameris, Bregt (2017) *Film Museum Practice and Film Historiography. The Case of the Nederlands Filmmuseum (1946-2000).* Amsterdam: Amsterdam University Press.

Lange, David (1982) 'Recognizing the Public Domain', *Law and Contemporary Problems*, 44(4), pp. 147-178.

Lessig, Lawrence (2001) *The Future of Ideas: The Fate of the Commons in a Connected World.* New York: Random House.

Lessig, Lawrence (2004) *Free Culture: How Big Media Uses Technology and the Law to Lock Down Culture and Control Creativity.* New York: The Penguin Press.

Lessig, Lawrence (2006) *Code: Version 2.0.* New York: Basic Books.

Lessig, Lawrence (2008) *Remix: Making Art and Commerce Thrive in the Hybrid Economy.* New York: The Penguin Press.

Lessig, Lawrence (2008) 'Little Orphan Artworks' [Op-Ed] *New York Times*, 20 May 2008.

Leyda, Jay (1964) *Films Beget Films. A Study of the Compilation Film.* New York: Hill and Wang.

Litman, Jessica (1990) 'The Public Domain', *Emory Law Journal*, 39 (L.J. 965), pp. 965-1023.

Library of Congress, National Recording Preservation Board (2010) *The State of Recorded Sound Preservation in the United States: A National Legacy at Risk in the Digital Age.* Washington, D.C.: Library of Congress. [Online]. Available at: http://www.loc.gov/rr/record/nrpb/pub148.pdf (accessed on 21 April 2016).

Loughney, Patrick (1988) *A Descriptive Analysis of the Library of Congress Paper Print Collection and Related Copyright Materials.* PhD Dissertation, George Washington University.

MacDonald, Scott (1988; 1992; 1998; 2004; 2006) *A Critical Cinema. Interviews With Independent Filmmakers.* Parts 1-5. Berkeley: University of California Press.

Manoff, Marlene (2004) 'Theories of the Archive from Across the Disciplines', *Libraries and the Academy*, 4(1), pp. 9-25.

Mashon, Mike (2013) 'Early Motion Pictures', *American Artifacts*, C-SPAN, 27 March [Online] Available at: http://www.c-span.org/video/?313371-1/early-motion-pictures (accessed on 12 November 2015).

Mazzanti, Nicola (ed.) (2011) *Digital Agenda for the European Film Heritage; Challenges of the Digital Era for Film Heritage Institutions*, Final Report prepared for the European Commission, DG Information Society and Media.

McCallum, Simon (Curator Mediathèque, British Film Institute) (2010) Interviewed by Claudy Op den Kamp, London, 26 October.

McCausland, Sally (2009) 'Getting Public Broadcaster Archives Online', *Media and Arts Law Review*, 14(2), pp. 142-165.

Melville, Annette, and Scott Simmon (1993) *Report of the Librarian of Congress. Film Preservation 1993. A Study of the Current State of American Film Preservation.* Washington, DC: Library of Congress [Online]. Available at: http://www.loc.gov/film/study.html (accessed on 21 April 2016).

Mendis, Dinusha (2016) 'Orphan Works', *copyrightuser*, available at: http://www.copyrightuser.org/understand/exceptions/orphan-works/ (accessed on 11 October 2017)

Meyer, Mark-Paul (2011) 'Authenticiteit en fotografische materialiteit', in Annemieke de Jong (ed.) *Zorgen voor onzichtbare assets. Over het behoud van digitale AV-collecties.* Hilversum: Beeld en Geluid, pp. 95–108.

Meyer, Mark-Paul (2012) 'From the Archive and Other Contexts', in Marente Bloemheuvel, Giovanna Fossati, and Jaap Guldemond (eds.) *Found Footage. Cinema Exposed.* Amsterdam: Amsterdam University Press/EYE Film Institute Netherlands, pp. 145–152.

Milestone Film & Video (2005) *BEYOND THE ROCKS* [Press release].

NFPF (ed.) (2004) *The Film Preservation Guide.* San Francisco: NFPF.

NYT (1988), 'Reagan Signs Law on Film', *New York Times*, 28 September 1988.

Netanel, Neil Weinstock (2008) *Copyright's Paradox.* New York: Oxford University Press.

Nissen, Dan (ed.) (2002) *Preserve Then Show.* Copenhagen: Danish Film Institute.

Noordegraaf, Julia (2010) 'Performing the Archive: Archivists as Editors of Knowledge', *Reimagining the Archive: Remapping and Remixing Traditional Models in the Digital Age*, University of California Los Angeles, Los Angeles, 12–14 November.

Olesen, Christian Gosvig (2013) 'Found Footage Photogénie: An Interview with Elif Rongen-Kaynakci and Mark-Paul Meyer', *Necsus, European Journal of Media Studies*, 4 [Online]. Available at: http://www.necsus-ejms.org/found-footage-photogenie-an-interview-with-elif-rongen-kaynakci-and-mark-paul-meyer/ (accessed on 21 April 2016).

Olesen, Christian Gosvig (2017) *Film History in the Making. Film Historiography, Digitised Archives and Digital Research Dispositifs.* PhD Dissertation, University of Amsterdam.

Osthoff, Simone (2009) *Performing the Archive: Transformation of the Archive in Contemporary Art from Repository of Documents to Art Medium.* New York: Atropos Press

Padfield, Tim (2010) 'Preserving and Accessing our Cultural Heritage – Issues for Cultural Sector Institutions: Archives, Libraries, Museums and Galleries', in Estelle Derclaye (ed.) *Copyright and Cultural Heritage. Preservation and Access to Works in a Digital World.* Cheltenham: Edward Elgar Publishing, pp. 195–209.

Padfield, Tim (2015) *Copyright for Archivists and Records Managers.* London: Facet Publishing.

Paletz, Gabriel (2001) 'Archives and Archivists Remade: The Paper Print Collection and The Film of Her', *The Moving Image*, 1(1), pp. 68–93.

Pallante, Maria (2012a) 'Orphan Works & Mass Digitization: Obstacles & Opportunities' [Keynote Address] *Berkeley Digital Copyright Project*, Berkeley Center for Law and Technology, 12 April 2012.

Pallante, Maria (2012b) 'Orphan Works and Mass Digitization', *Federal Register*, 77(204), Washington, DC: Library of Congress, Copyright Office, pp. 64555–64561.

Parker, Mark, and Deborah Parker (2011) *The DVD and the Study of Film. The Attainable Text*. New York: Palgrave MacMillan.

Patterson, Kerry, Ronan Deazley, and Victoria Stobo (2016) *Digitising the Edwin Morgan Scrapbooks: Diligent Search in Context and Practice*. Glasgow: CREATe. Available at: http://www.digitisingmorgan.org/uploads/DILIGENCE_SECTION_DigiMorgan.pdf (accessed on 11 October 2017).

Patry, William (2009) *Moral Panics and the Copyright Wars*. New York: Oxford University Press.

Pierce, David (2007) 'Forgotten Faces: Why Some of Our Cinema Heritage Is Part of the Public Domain', *Film History*, 19, pp. 125–143.

Pierce, David (2013) *The Survival Rate of American Silent Feature Films 1912-1929*. Washington, DC: Library of Congress. Available at: https://www.loc.gov/programs/static/national-film-preservation-board/documents/pub158.final_version_sept_2013.pdf (accessed on 27 September 2017).

Prelinger, Rick (2010) 'Points of Origin. Discovering Ourselves Through Access', *The Moving Image*, 9(2), pp. 164–175.

Punt, Michael (2000) *Early Cinema and the Technological Imaginary*. PhD Dissertation, University of Amsterdam.

Read, Paul, and Mark-Paul Meyer (eds.) (2000) *Restoration of Motion Picture Film*. Oxford: Butterworth-Heinemann.

Rechsteiner, Emjay (Curator Contemporary Dutch Film, Eye Film Institute Netherlands) (2010) Interviewed by Claudy Op den Kamp. Philadelphia, US, 6 November.

Roberts, Helene (1994) 'Second Hand Images: The Role of Surrogates in Artistic and Cultural Exchange', *Visual Resources*, 9(4), pp. 335–346.

Rother, Rainer (2014) *Filmhistorisches Arbeiten am Museum* [Lecture Forschungskolloquium FIWI, University of Zurich]. 15 October.

Roud, Richard (1983) *A Passion for Films: Henri Langlois and the Cinémathèque Française*. New York: The Viking Press.

Russell, Patrick (2013) 'Re:found footage', *www.bfi.org.uk* [Online]. Available at: http://www.bfi.org.uk/news-opinion/bfi-news/re-found-footage (accessed on 21 April 2016).

Samuelson, Pamela (2003) 'Mapping the Public Domain', *Law and Contemporary Problems*, 66(147), pp. 147–171.

Schoots, Hans (2004) *Van Fanfare tot Spetters. Een cultuurgeschiedenis van de jaren zestig en zeventig*. Amsterdam: Uitgeverij Bas Lubberhuizen.

Slave to the rhythm. Christian Marclay on deadline (2010) Available at: http://www.economist.com/node/16885826 (accessed on 16 October 2017)

Slide, Anthony (1992) *Nitrate Won't Wait: A History of Film Preservation in the United States*. Jefferson: McFarland & Company.

Stobo, Victoria, Ronan Deazley, and Ian Anderson (2013) *Copyright & Risk: Scoping the Wellcome Digital Library Project*. CREATe Working Paper No.10. Glasgow: University of Glasgow.

Strauven, Wanda (2013) 'Media Archaeology: Where Film History, Media Art, and New Media (Can) Meet', in Julia Noordegraaf, Cosetta Saba, Barbara Le Maitre, and Vinzenz Hediger (eds.) *Preserving and Exhibiting Media Art. Challenges and Perspectives*. Amsterdam: Amsterdam University Press.

Streible, Dan (2009) 'The State of Orphan Films: Editor's Introduction', *The Moving Image, Special Issue on Orphan Film*, 9(1), pp. vi-xix.

Swanson, Gloria (1980) *Swanson on Swanson*. New York: Random House.

Testa, Bart (1992) *Back and Forth: Early Cinema and the Avant-Garde*. Waterloo, Ontario: Wilfrid Laurier University Press.

Thompson, Kristin (2007) 'The Celestial Multiplex', *Observations on Film Art* [Online]. Available at: http://www.davidbordwell.net/blog/2007/03/27/the-celestial-multiplex/ (accessed on 21 April 2016).

Thouvenel, Eric (2008) 'How Found Footage Made me Think Twice About Film History', *Cinéma & Cie*, 10, pp. 97–103.

Townsend Gard, Elizabeth (2017) 'J.D. Salinger and Copyright's Rule of the Shorter Term', *Vanderbilt Journal of Entertainment & Technology Law*, 19, pp. 777-815.

Twining, William (2008) 'Law in Context Movement', in Peter Cane and Joanne Conaghan (eds.) *The New Oxford Companion to Law*. Oxford: Oxford University Press.

UNITED NATIONS EDUCATIONAL SCIENTIFIC AND CULTURAL ORGANIZATION (UNESCO) (1991) *Legal Questions Facing Audiovisual Archives*. Paris: UNESCO [Online]. Available at: unesdoc.unesco.org/images/0008/000886/088674e.pdf (accessed on 21 April 2016).

United States Copyright Office (USCO) (1989) Technological Alterations to Motion Pictures and Other Audiovisual Works: Implications for Creators, Copyright Owners and Consumers. Report of the Register of Copyrights. [Online]. Available at: http://digitalcommons.lmu.edu/elr/vol10/iss1/1/ (accessed on 10 March 2015).

United States Copyright Office (USCO) (2006) *Report on Orphan Works*. Washington: Library of Congress.

Vaidhyanathan, Siva (2001) *Copyrights and Copywrongs: the Rise of Intellectual Property and how it Threatens Creativity*. New York: NYU Press.

Vaidhyanathan, Siva (2017) *Intellectual Property. A Very Short Introduction*. Oxford: Oxford University Press.

van Driel, Anne (2003) 'Ach, zo'n gerucht doet het goed voor de film', *de Volkskrant,* 23 August 2003.

van Gompel, Stef (2007a) 'Audiovisual Archives and the Inability to Clear Rights in Orphan Works', *IRIS Plus, a supplement to IRIS, Legal Observations of the European Audiovisual Observatory*, 04, pp. 1–8.

van Gompel, Stef (2007b) 'Unlocking the Potential of Pre-Existing Content: How to Address the Issue of Orphan Works in Europe?', *IIC*, 6/2007, pp. 669-702.

van Gompel, Stef (2011) *Formalities in Copyright Law. An Analysis of Their History, Rationales and Possible Future.* PhD thesis, University of Amsterdam.

van Gompel, Stef, and Bernt Hugenholtz (2010) 'The Orphan Works Problem: The Copyright Conundrum of Digitizing Large-Scale Audiovisual Archives, and How to Solve It', *Popular Communication. The International Journal of Media and Culture*, 8(1), pp. 61–71.

Verhoeff, Nanna (2006) *The West in Early Cinema. After the Beginning.* Amsterdam: Amsterdam University Press.

Vetulani, Agnieszka (2008) *The Problem of Orphan Works in the EU.* Brussels: European Commission.

Vicki Bennett's The Zone *withdrawn from circulation* (2013) Available at: https://www.thewire.co.uk/news/22362/vicki-bennett_s-the-zone-withdrawn-from-circulation (accessed on 16 October 2017)

Vooren, Géraldine (2011) 'Film Clearing in Practice', *European Film Gateway Symposium, Taking Care of Orphan Works*, EYE, Amsterdam, 31 May.

Vooren, Géraldine (2014) 'Project forward: Legal Rescue of Orphan Works', *9th Orphan Film Symposium*, EYE, Amsterdam, 2 April.

VPRO, 2004. RAM [television programme]. NL3. 18 April 2004.

Wall, Jayson (2011) 'Restoring Nothing Sacred (US 1937, William Wellman)', *AMIA Archival Screening Night*, 17 November.

Wallace, Andrea (2015) 'Surrogate Rights Explained', *www.surrogateiprights.org*, available at: http://surrogateiprights.org/surrogate-rights-explained/ (accessed on 14 October 2017)

Wallace, Andrea (2016) 'Cultural Institutions and Surrogate Intellectual Property Rights: Resisting an Artwork's Transfer into the Public Domain', *ISHTIP conference*, University of Glasgow, 6–8 July.

Walls, Howard (1953) *Motion Pictures 1894-1912. Identified from the Records of the United States Copyright Office.* Washington DC: Library of Congress Copyright Office.

Wees, William (1993) *Recycled Images: The Art and Politics of Found Footage Films.* New York: Anthology Film Archives.

Welsch, Tricia (2013) *Gloria Swanson. Ready for her Close-Up.* Jackson: University Press of Mississippi.

Welgraven, Co (2001) '...ging ALS TWEE DRUPPELS WATER achter slot en grendel',
     Trouw, 26 March.
Wipp, Glenn (2014) '"L.A. PLAYS ITSELF" is finally coming to home video. Here's how',
     Los Angeles Times, 26 July.
World Intellectual Property Organization (WIPO) (2001) *Intellectual Property
     Handbook: Policy, Law and Use*, Geneva: World Intellectual Property Organization.
Zalewski, Daniel (2012) 'The Hours; How Christian Marclay made the Ultimate Digital
     Mosaic', *The New Yorker*, March 12. [Online]. Available at: http://www.newyorker.
     com/magazine/2012/03/12/the-hours-2 (accessed on 21 April 2016).

INDEX